The Musician's Breath

THE ROLE OF BREATHING IN HUMAN EXPRESSION

The Companion DVD

THE MUSICIAN'S BREATH
MARK MOLITERNO
WITH
JAMES JORDAN
NOVA THOMAS

The Musician's Breath

THE ROLE OF BREATHING IN HUMAN EXPRESSION

JAMES JORDAN

WITH

MARK MOLITERNO
NOVA THOMAS

GIA PUBLICATIONS, INC.
CHICAGO

Wisdom is the principal thing, therefore get wisdom:
and with all thy getting get understanding.

—Proverbs 4:7

The larger the island of knowledge
the greater the shoreline of wonder. (p. 109)

—Huston Smith
in William Sloan Coffin, *Credo*

The Musician's Breath:
The Role of Breathing in Human Expression
James Jordan

Art direction/design & illustrations: Martha Chlipala

G-7955
ISBN: 978-1-57999-834-9
Copyright © 2011 GIA Publications, Inc.
7404 S. Mason Avenue, Chicago, Illinois 60638

GIA Publications, Inc.
www.giamusic.com

To: Morten Johannes Lauridsen...

My good friend whose music has inspired us through sound, for all to ponder breath and all its miracles within and among the notes he sets to paper.

— James Jordan

Contents

PART I
THE POWER OF THE BREATH

PART II
INTERPRETATIONS AND APPLICATIONS

Foreword

What you do is what the whole universe is doing at the place you call "here and now," and you are something the whole universe is doing in the same way that a wave is something that the whole ocean is doing. (p. 73)

—Alan Watts
"Man in Nature" from *The Tao of Philosophy* in Yi-Fu Tuan,
Religion: From Place to Placelessness

It is clear that respiration has its source from within, whether we are right to describe it as a function of the soul or the soul itself or else by some mixture of bodies which by their means causes this attraction. (p. 497)

—Aristotle
in *On Breath*

ACKNOWLEDGING A SIMPLER TRUTH

There are certain truths in art and artistic expression. It seems almost like a rite of passage for artists that we must submerge ourselves in the complexities of our art to begin to be able to acknowledge and, yes, accept some basic simple truths. Some of those truths are acknowledged, some are avoided, and others are hidden from our view. Obscured by detail and technique, we struggle throughout our careers to find "answers." Often, it is always the obvious things—the simple truths—that are the hardest to recognize, and even harder to acknowledge because they are just that: simple. It is much easier for us to hide behind and reason in complex terms rather than yield (even submit) ourselves to an idea that is beautifully simple and direct. It seems too simple to be true.

This book is ultimately about a simple truth for all musicians: that the breath is the most magical and human thing we can engage as artists. Breath is the only vehicle we have for the transport of human idea and human spirit. To deny the power of breath is to deny one the ability to be truly expressive and honest in all things musical. Music without breath as a carrier of human expression is at most a contrivance and at worst something slightly dishonest that never quite communicates the human idea at hand.

To understand its power is, in a way, to yield to an idea and truth bigger than any one of us that, when acknowledged, can provide a musical threshold and entrance into the miracle of human expression in sound. The intent of this book is to convince you of the powers of the breath and encourage you to submit yourself to its miracles. By allowing yourself enough vulnerability to yield to the powers of inhalation and exhalation, you realize how artistic expression within the human being defies a great deal of objective logic. Breath holds the key for all musicians. A yielding through understanding of its inherent magic is the purpose of this book.

Breath is such a simple concept that it is elusive. It seems too simple to hold the answers to our art, but the truth is…it does. Aristotle devoted an entire volume of thought to what breath does in defining the human experience. If Aristotle could grapple with its mysteries,[1] then shouldn't we as musicians come to terms with its profound magic? Allow your breath to work its miracle upon your music.

TRACING STEPS

I was trying to remember when I first became aware of breath and its importance for my work as a conductor. I remember vividly in graduate school that almost every lesson in my first year of study with Elaine Brown addressed either the mechanics of breathing as a conductor or how the breath is connected to opening and vulnerability. I also remember that while Dr. Brown continually insisted on my breathing as a conductor, I really never fully grasped in my lessons its full importance—and the gift she gave me. So many years later, that teaching has come full circle.

I do remember, however, my understanding began one day in a Temple Concert Choir rehearsal with Dr. Brown. We were rehearsing Aaron Copland's *In the Beginning*. For those of you who may be familiar with the work, the final passage has clearly delineated breaths marked by the composer indicated below by (*):

---

1   Aristotle's in-depth discussion on breath can be found in Book VIII, Part III, titled *On Breath*.

And Breathed into his Nostrils(*)
The breath of Life (*)
And Man became a living SOUL! (*)
And Man became a living SOUL! (*)
A Living (*)
SOUL! (*)

I remember as if it were yesterday Dr. Brown's meticulous work to get us to breathe not only together but also on the depth of the breath and its ability to carry the miracle of the idea of the text. She talked about the enormity of the human message and how the breath is the only way to not only communicate but also connect. I profoundly remember how moved we all were that day, and from that day forward when we performed that piece. There is no doubt in my mind that Copland's use of breaths strategically planted points for singers to breathe the almost overwhelming human ideas into that great text. I still remember Dr. Brown conducting that specific passage, and how that day changed my idea about the power of breath that brought me to write this book.

Dr. Brown always told us that great ideas should not be held—they should be shared. She also told us that choirs "sing as they are able to sing." I never quite understood then why the choirs I sang in with her had such power, honesty, and beauty. I know that her almost intuitive sense of the power of the breath, which I believe she learned from John Finley Williamson, was the key that unlocked the scores we sang and revealed the human messages contained within those scores. This book is my attempt after all these years to draw conductors and musicians to this miracle, to underline its almost singular importance in human expression, and to convince you of its necessity.

I was originally considering a book pertaining to the breath and its relationship to conducting. But like so many things in my career, there were several serendipitous events that ignited this book, the strongest of which was a masterclass by Thomas Hampson that I attended in November 2009. That masterclass reconnected and reaffirmed within me with some basic truths about music making and artistry. Mr. Hampson's elegant and passionate language about breath was one of the major sparks for this book. I cannot thank him enough for his teaching that day.

I have several other persons to thank as well. Obviously, without Elaine Brown, this conductor would have never been led to breath and its powers. To Edwin Gordon, my doctoral advisor, who has been preaching the power of what he calls "the audiational breath." As he has done with so many other ideas, Dr. Gordon has tried to get us to understand how breath and audiation are intimately related. I carry his teachings and his ideas with me daily. Lynn Eustis, who began as my student teacher many years ago and has been my friend all these years. An artist-teacher in her own right, Dr. Eustis read this manuscript, edited it a bit, and offered valuable insights that I incorporated into the book. Her insights can be seen in the Study Guide to be used with this book. Thanks also to my friend Father Mark Kelleher, who provided some additional insights and connections for this book.

I am so fortunate to be at Westminster Choir College and have colleagues that inspire me daily. I asked Mark Moliterno and Nova Thomas to be part of this book, not only because of the insights they could bring to help convince and clarify but also because I hear what they teach in the sounds of the singers who come from their studios.

They are master teachers and artists both, and I deeply cherish their friendship and artistry as teachers.

And as always, my editor Linda Vickers and Martha Chlipala, the graphic artist who provides the visual support for these powerful ideas. With them, this book has become a reality. My deepest thanks to them.

And one more thank you. Weston Noble has been a friend and an inspiration for many years. His affirmation of me and the ideas contained within have given me the tenacity to find the words to describe this miracle.

—James Jordan

Yardley, Pennsylvania

Prologue

THE THING ITSELF

On a dark day I will become nearly overwhelmed at how little I have mastered in my life. Starting a new piece can cause me torment and can mean having to slog through a dismal swamp of indifferent ideas, pushing them, prodding them, often abandoning them in disgust or desperation. (p. 311)

—John Adams
in *Hallelujah Junction*

John of Forde knows only too well the dangers of those who 'are so entirely given over to exterior concerns' that they can scarcely 'endure taking a deep breath in the depths of their souls or ever recollecting themselves.' (p. 159)

—Ester DeWaal
in *The Way of Simplicity*

But whatever the form the composer chooses to adopt, there
is always one great desideratum: The form must have what
in my student days we used to call *la grande ligne* (the long
line). It is difficult adequately to explain the meaning of that
phrase to the layman. To be properly understood in relation
to a piece of music, it must be felt. In mere words, it simply
means that every good piece of music must give us a sense
of flow—a sense of continuity from first note to last. Every
elementary music student knows the principle, but to put it
into practice has challenged the greatest minds in music! A
great symphony is a man-made Mississippi down which we
irresistibly flow from the instant of our leave-taking to a long
foreseen destination. Music must always flow, for that is part
of its very essence, but the creation of that continuity and
flow—that long line—constitutes the be-all and end-all of
every composer's existence. (pp. 26–27)

—Aaron Copland
in *What to Listen for in Music*

A rigorous and unassailable code, but there are corollaries
and codicils even to it, I think. The stark judgment of the
moment is a rigor meant for oneself alone, not for others.
Basic human decency argues against it. What we mean by
compassion is often just that sympathetic imagination for how
people got where they are, and that belief in their possibilities
for change. And there is another caveat: occasionally we do
grant to ourselves, having felt some mercy from a source
unknown, the possibility of redemption. (p. 238)

—Richard Todd
in *The Thing Itself*

2

It seems to me I've interviewed a lot of singers lately who love to golf. What is the connection there? I think there is a connection. There are tremendous parallels between shaping your shots and finding your inner rhythm to singing. One of the first things a golf pro said to me when I was first golfing was, "You don't breathe when you golf." And then as the game went on and I realized that I was really not breathing, he said, "OK, now that I've solved that, would you teach me how to breathe?" It was an amazing conversation. It depends what level you're playing at. With real golfers like Barbara Bonney, Ferruccio Furlanetto, Paul Groves, your game becomes one of visualizing shots and setting up the technical aspects of your swing, releasing all of that, and simply going to the shot. That's a perfect description of singing. If you don't hear it before you sing it, you're probably not going to sing it the way you want it to be sung. The most profoundly simple mandate I can give to any singer is, "Hear it, breathe into that which you are going to make audible, and sing!"... You can only play your game. You can't go and try to swing somebody off the course, and that's very true in singing as well: You must remain true to yourself.

—Thomas Hampson
in "Playing Your Game"
San Francisco Classical Voice
September 29, 2009

So after a point has ended and I'm returning to position or going to pick up a ball, I place my mind on my breathing. The second my mind starts wondering about whether I'm going to win or lose the match, I bring it gently back to my breath and relax in its natural and basic motion. In this way, by the time the next point is ready to start, I am able to be more concentrated than I was in the midst of the previous one. (p. 97)

—W. Timothy Gallwey
from *The Inner Game of Tennis*

The idea of breath in and of itself seems both simple and blatantly obvious. To say that musicians should breathe seems to be an obvious "given." In fact, it is such a given that perhaps conductors take it for granted. While singers and instrumentalists are less inclined to do so because it is the breath that runs the instruments, conductors and collaborative musicians might not fully grasp the power they hold, which is contained in an understanding of not only *how* to breathe but *what* to breathe. In the first quote above, composer John Adams remarks that on days he becomes overwhelmed with how little he has mastered in his life. For me, there are days as a conductor when I feel the same way regarding breath and its almost magical and mystical ability to influence all that follows, whether it be tone, musical gesture, or profound human idea. While my teacher told me of the power of the breath, and I sort of "did it," I have spent the last thirty years pondering its many faceted miracles and mysteries, and I have both struggled with and marveled over its miracles. Breathing is indeed a miracle, and for musicians it carries almost magical and clairvoyant qualities.

The goal of this book is to convince you (perhaps for the first time) of the power breath contains with every inhalation and expiration, and to also guide you to ways in which you can allow air to enter your body in a deep and profound way. Without breath, our truly human ideas are never given flight. Without breath empowered with purpose or intention, our best musical intentions and human ideas will only rise to the level of veiled and muddled sounds that have limited communication potential for our art.

DEFINING THE ISSUES AND THE IDEAS

Many students I have worked with seem to understand intellectually why breath is important, and they believe that they do breathe. But when we focus on the process and its products, the students often raise the following arguments:

- Being in the moment has nothing to do with breath.

- Breath just happens; no special effort needs to be made to breathe. After all, we breathe to live. What's the difference?

- The only function of breath is to run the sound-producing apparatus.

- (*on the part of those who conduct*) Breath has no influence over either the sound of the ensemble or the musical intent at hand.

- Breath does not carry or is incapable of carrying interpretive ideas.

- Breath does not initiate or carry musical idea.

- It is possible to connect and communicate with ensembles and other musicians without breath; musicianship and interpretative ideas can be read through other means.

- Eyes have no connection with breath; they are able to function independently as an expressive device.

- Color and texture changes can be effected in an ensemble without breath or breathing on the part of the conductor.

If a musician commits to breathing and realizes its importance through thought and study, then the following problems may arise:

- Body rigidity blocks the power of the breath.

- The body is unable to open to allow breath in.

- Getting breath into the body is challenging if not impossible.

- Breath does not fall into the body in a wavelike motion from top to bottom.

- The musical idea is not infused into the breath at the moment of inspiration.

- The musical idea is carried into music through good intention alone. Breath is expendable in the process of music making.

- Musicians are unable to release musical idea into the breath and allow the breath to carry the message and the story of the music.

- Musicians are unable to trust others to respond to the breath.

- Breath is not a key for any *connection* to others or deeper understanding in the musicing process.

- It is difficult, if not impossible, for the breath to be deep within the body.

- Musicians want to breathe and believe that they do, but their breath does not compel others to do likewise.

- There is a lack of understanding that breath inhabits a sacred space within us and that space must be prepared for the breath to take inhabitance.

- Breath does not grow out of profound stillness and inward awareness.

- Breath is not part of the connective tissue that connects the physical actions of our bodies and the intent of our spirit.[1]

These are the most common issues to be dealt with when beginning one's understanding of the breath as discussed in this book.

I love the title of one of the final chapters of John Adams' book *Hallelujah Junction* entitled "Yard Sale of the Mind." At first glance, the list above may appear to be a "yard sale" of interesting points, which implies you can pick and choose. While this may seem at the outset of your breath journey to be an odd collection of ideas, you must overcome *all* of these issues, not just some of them, to gain complete understanding and intimate ownership of the principles presented in this text. Acceptance of these ideas is not optional;

---

[1] The term "connective tissue" is used by co-author Mark Moliterno in describing that link in oneself between the physical and spiritual. His use of this term is explained in Chapter 14 and on the companion DVD to this book.

these ideas must become a canon of one's very mode of musical and human operation. The acceptance of the role of breath as presented herein will move the philosophical concept of breath to a living part of your musicing...the connective tissue in all that you do and all that you are.

The role of this book is to convince you of the power you have in your own breath (or re-orient you to this power). To simply allude to the power of breath makes a smoke-and-mirrors operation of all we do as musicians. If we wish our music to be compelling and life affirming, then breath and the profound understanding of its powers must be deeply ingrained in both psyche and soul. In the most profound way, breathing is the *only* way "in" for musicians to visit an idea before giving birth to the idea in sound; it is also the only way musicians and artists can connect with themselves. It is not only our connective tissue but also our transport vehicle. It is breath that connects blood to bone, and spirit to idea. Breath allows us to occasion our ideas more intimately and more profoundly. Breath is the only way to touch a "realm" of profound creativity. It is the breath that makes our ideas fertile. We must "re-language" how we access the breath and infuse that breath with idea. Breath, in the words of The Beatles, is quite the *Magical Mystery Tour*. Enjoy, be fascinated, and bask in what will be a first-time experience with this wonder of our art.

PART I

THE POWER OF THE BREATH

CHAPTER 1

TO HEAR THE INAUDIBLE

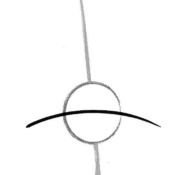

You don't have to justify what is in that space before you speak.

—M. C. Richards
in *The Fire Within*

Inspirit 1. To put spirit, life, or energy into; to quicken, enliven, animate, to incite, stir.

—The Compact Edition of
the Oxford English
Dictionary

I would like to encourage you never sing to anyone, and you certainly never sing at anyone. You do, however, sing for them in the sense that you let them hear what you are thinking. And what you're thinking is what you're re-creating, which has already been thought.

It just gets less and less about you every minute, doesn't it? It isn't about us....EVER. It's about what we're singing. You should never come out on stage with something to say. They have come to be part of your life.

Now the interesting thing about singing is when we have the need or the desire to make audible this thing that goes on forever. I promise you, technically, ALL you want to think about is inhaling. Just keep the feeling of drawing in the breath while you are singing, and make your thoughts audible. Three things I want you to know today. The first is your mantra for the rest of your life: Hear it; I mean hear it exactly how you want it to be heard in every aspect.

You hear THAT, you breathe into THAT, and you make THAT audible.

> —Thomas Hampson
> from a masterclass at
> Westminster Choir
> College
> November 19, 2009

You must work out of your own silence. Not knowing and trusting simultaneously.

> —M. C. Richards
> in *The Fire Within*

Thus, the story of Adam and Eve is not about sin, disobedience, sex, or shame, but is an attempt to explain the reality of death. The first lesson in this tradition having to do with living the good life is that life, however good, is finite, a limited resource, and that one does not have all the time in the world to discover what it is or how to live it. The first duty of self-awareness, therefore, is the knowledge of the fewness of one's days. (p. 136)

—Peter Gomes
in *The Good Life*

"Would you tell me please," said Alice, "what that means?" "Now you talk like a reasonable child," said Humpty Dumpty, looking very much pleased. "I meant by impenetrability that we've had enough of that subject, and it would be just as well if you'd mention what you mean to do next, as I suppose you don't mean to stop here the rest of your life."

—Lewis Carroll
in *Through the Looking Glass*

Imaginative people trick their brains all the time. That's how they accomplish their dreams. And brains love it. They're in the game-playing business. They'll play games with you if you don't give them something to do. (p. 1)

Off-stage you are in your own private world. On stage is a public world. To perform, you have to get from one world to the other. Between these two worlds you are nowhere—no longer where you were and not yet where you're going. I call this in-between area "no-man's land." (p. 113)

—Michael Colgrass
in *My Lessons with Kumi*

Breath

    Breathing

        Inspiration

            Expiration

                Expression

These are not words that are unfamiliar to any musician. We all use them in our daily teaching, and we certainly have come to some technical common ground (we think) on the role that breath plays in the production of musical sound. But I recently have become fascinated with the other things our breath carries. I have talked about the importance of breath in the musicing process and written about it in a cursory way. But after being forced to take a closer look, I am astounded by the power of breath and the implications for deepening our musicing.   I have started to "connect the dots." While I know all of the dots, and have even labeled them in a kind of pedagogical process, a clear and vivid picture has eluded me and, I suspect, many others (including my own students). Aside from carrying the more mundane matters of musicing, tempo, color of sound, and dynamic, *breath* is a vehicle for so much more if we give ourselves a bit of time to contemplate its miracles and have the courage to empower it.

The late Robert Shaw talked of the silent power of breathing. To paraphrase Mr. Shaw, breath goes in and out of us constantly, even as we sleep. It is never interrupted, and we need to acknowledge that it *is,* or rather can be, a carrier of the musical idea.

In fact, the point I attempt to make is that it is the *only* carrier of musical idea and human expression.

The intent of this book is to find common ground in understanding, at least on a basic level, how the miracle of sound becomes bonded to human thought and idea. While thought and human emotion are partly born in one's cognitive thought, those profoundly human emotions and ideas are delivered to audiences by way of sound, but are transported into the sounds we make by our breath. Breath is the DNA of human expression. It is a silent transport system for all that we wish to communicate; it is all that we are. If we give the idea of breath at its most organic level its pedagogical due, our refocused attention on what we breathe *into* our own breath will for some of us profoundly deepen our musicing and for others begin to open a door to human expression that heretofore has been mentioned but certainly not discussed as a major channel into the complexities of the human soul and its expression in sound.

Great performing artists intuitively know these things presented in these pages. And we all have suspected at times in our own teaching and musicing that these "truths" about breath do exist. But breath and breathing (and their combined inherent power) have not been adopted on a widespread basis as *the* vehicle by teachers, music educators, conductors, and performers in general. While breathing processes are alluded to in many lessons, the miracles of breath are seldom discussed. Most of us have acknowledged in a passing way that breath is indeed important. But have we ever given breath its due? We understand its necessity perhaps, but do we really understand its power?

This book will not provide solutions, nor will it provide a specific pedagogy for achieving a type of artistic clairvoyance and expressive clarity that I hope to reignite through an understanding of breath. While I have a great and abiding belief in the power of pedagogy and process, the moment that defines artistic creation *defies process*, and we must accept that as both teachers and performers. An awareness of breath's power to communicate and connect is what I hope to convey and, perhaps, even clarify a bit. I also hope to provide several doors through which you can enter into a deeper expressive dimension, through breath, towards what we all want and deeply desire in our teaching and our doing—that is, to transport those very ideas through the dimensions of breath, which makes us human to those who listen to our message through sound. Such is the stuff of authentic and deeply honest communication.

CHAPTER 2

The Ignorance of Breath

Out of deep breathing issue physical and psychic energies.
(p. 17)

> —Wilhelm Ehmann
> in *Choral Directing*

The building blocks of text, rhythm, and pitch we have been discussing are here woven into one whole: the song itself. The basic unit of the combination is the phrase, the smallest element of musical thought. Just as in the English language, the phrase expresses an idea, and several phrases can make up the equivalent of a sentence or a paragraph.

Phrases begin and end with an intake of breath, and their length is often determined by this physical limitation. Breath is to the singer as the floor is to the dancer. There is no way to escape this human necessity. It is woven into the fabric of all song. (p. 67)

> —Alice Parker
> in *The Anatomy of
> Melody*

Mirror Neurons in your mind have "emotional" content.

I must fire your neurons as a conductor and that can only be done through the breath! We have not even begun to discover the treasures in our breath as conductors!

—Weston Noble
at The Westminster
Conducting Institute
June 29, 2010

The connections which I want particularly to celebrate here today are those between the inner invisible realm of the "force" and the outer visible realm of the "flower," the inner realm of nature and the inner realm of man, connections between the invisible life of man and the invisible life of the universe, invisible that is to ordinary eyesight. Connections between human beings, between fields of study and work, the fabric of a common spiritual community. Artists are sometimes particularly attuned to these connections, scientists too, mystics too, soul-brothers too. (p. 171)

—M. C. Richards
in *The Crossing Point*

Therefore, the basic trick is in the preparatory upbeat. It is exactly like breathing: the preparation is like an inhalation, and the music sounds like an exhalation. We all have to inhale in order to speak, for example; all verbal expression is exhaled. So it is with music: we inhale on the upbeat and sing out a phrase of music, then inhale again and breathe out the next phrase. A conductor who breathes with the music has gone far in acquiring a technique. (p. 272)

—Leonard Bernstein
in Carl Bamberger,
The Conductor's Art

Allow me a small digression and a bit of introspection. I have always been deeply concerned, and a bit puzzled, when I encounter musicians (especially conductors) who do not breathe during their musicing. What I hear is music that not only lacks a sonic dimensionality and richness, but also carries a muted or very murky interpretative message. Without the engagement of the breath in the musicing process, the sounds that follow always seem to be a bit labored and thin, and the sounds seemed handicapped and unable to carry meaningful human emotion or to communicate anything to anyone. Moreover, conductors who do not breathe usually are severely limited in the colors they can achieve with their ensembles. In most cases, the sound of those ensembles is monochromatic, robbing the conductors of an expressive device. Changes in style, therefore, can only be accomplished by focusing on articulation instead of articulation *and* color.

Elaine Brown, my teacher, always asked her students to make music that was "meaningful." As a young conductor, I thought meaningful music was that music born out of intense and sequestered score study—understanding phrase structure, harmonic motion and such. Those elements of a musician's preparation are indeed important. But the meaningful issue is: How does one make one's music making meaningful. M. C. Richards, in her book, *The Moral Eye,* speaks of the importance of authenticity and honesty in artistic creation. She says she knows that art will live with those characteristics when there is true "spiritual presence" in sound, word, or sight. It seems the challenge for all of us who conduct, teach, and perform is how to ensure that these mystical, almost clairvoyant qualities are in our musicing. Emphasis on the delivery system for all things human does not, in most cases, occupy a significant part of our creative thought, creative psyche, or our creative doing.

In a *New York Times*[2] review of a performance of *The Wound Dresser* (1988) for orchestra and baritone, the composer, John Adams, is quoted as saying, "In an astute description of the poem in a program note, Mr. Adams calls it the most intimate, graphic and profoundly affecting evocation of the act of nursing he knows of, a text 'astonishingly free of any kind of hyperbole or amplified emotion,' yet filled with imagery 'of a procession that only could be attained by one who had been there." The review continues:

> "Bearing the Bandages, water and sponge, Straight and
> swift to my wounded I go," he sings. As the description

---

2   Anthony Tomasini, "Poetry for Times of Calamity and War," C1, *The New York Times,* January 16, 2010.

of the scene becomes rawer, the music shifts from meditative restraint through restless agitation to controlled intensity. Now and then you hear a consoling battlefield trumpet. The music is driven by Whitman's words, set with a deft blend of achieving lyricism and conversational naturalness. Mr. Hampson brought myriad colorings to his singing—an almost spectral tone to convey the image of blood that 'reddens the grass, the ground,' and the plaintive beauty touched with longing when the poet describes the 'burning flame' he feels as he tends to soldier amputees who dare not look at their stumps. (p. C7)

Given the review above, and the music the composer wrote to carry the text, how then is it that we as musicians arrive at an "interpretation?" How is it that we set about doing what that composer has charged us with?How do we communicate the human message within the text?

All music, if it is worth "doing," carries profound human messages within its words sung or its sounds played. Those messages, when understood by performers and teachers, give interiority to art...profound human expression. Those messages must be sought and studied both through the words and the notes of the composer. Then after what I refer to as a moment of clairvoyance, where one understands in the most profound human way the "meaning," then it is the job of the performers to transport that message to others.

Many believe that an understanding and "interpretation" of the text is sufficient. I also believed that for many years and used that as my mode of operation. I thought that the sheer act of score study allowed me to somehow, magically, transport the message. What I failed to see was that while my understanding is an important step in the interpretative process, if I do nothing further, then the message is held *within* me. The experience of the performance in this case would be solely mine. The listener would somehow distill what I had been feeling, but just knowing a translation or "knowing" an interpretation of the words does not magically communicate those ideas to an ensemble or an audience. How does one first have a point of view, and further, how does one *convey* that point of view?

What I failed to understand for so many years is that the only vehicle for the transport of the deepest and most profound musical idea is breath. After one understands the physical process of breathing, and one understands that breath is taken during a state of intense vulnerability (to be explained in this book), then one must buy into the concept that it is only through breath that human spirit can be transported into the musicing process. Breath is the only way to carry the message. You cannot inflict interpretation of message while executing a phrase. *The phrase must be uploaded before any sound is made through and in the breath.* Breath transports the idea from conductor to ensemble, and breath likewise transports the idea from player or singer to listening audience. Every breath in a piece must be viewed as an opportunity for expression and transmission of the idea at the moment. You cannot will a musical idea—you must breathe the idea, and then the musicing takes care of itself.

We must hold ourselves to a higher standard as artists to breathe ideas, not just think them. It is your breath that will make your musicing honest, even meaningful. The intention of your breath is far more important than any physical gesture or facial expression. Through your breath, you can achieve and experience musical clairvoyance. If you can recall a musical performance where you felt the music was dull, listless, and its message veiled, most likely you did not empower your breath to do its work. When you overlook the power of the breath, you try to will the sounds you make; you tend to *make sound* instead of *allowing sound to happen*. Breaths are taken because they must be taken, but they are never empowered or *inspirited*. Don't underestimate the power of your breath to transport, transform and, at times, even be redemptive for your expressive lives. Breath, when viewed from this perspective in the musicing process, will refine your awareness and bring you into a deeper, more profound, and more meaningful relationship with the composer's intent.

CHAPTER 3

THE CLAIRVOYANT BREATH:
THE MOMENT OF CHOICE

Tap into your silence. Listening and receiving…you are empty in a way so that the impulse has someplace to enter. Let the ear be your main organ.

—M. C. Richards
in *The Fire Within*

For a composition is, after all, an organism. It is a living, not a static, thing. That is why it is capable of being seen in a different light and from different angles by various interpreters or even by the same interpreter at different times. Interpretation is, to a large extent, a matter of emphasis. Every piece has an essential quality which the interpretation must not betray. (p. 225)

—Aaron Copland
in *What to Listen for in Music*

At the macroscopic level, the brain—like the body—is a structure with a remarkable degree of bilateral symmetry. The mind, however, has but a single stream of consciousness, not two. (p. 294)

—Christof Koch
in *The Quest for
Consciousness*

On the subject of air, teachers of breathing tell me they enjoy far more success with their students when they are very clear in their language, particularly when they distinguish air and breath. Air is a substance which occupies the planet along with us. Breath is a reflexive human movement that allows us to move air in and out of our bodies, and the air goes only into our lungs through a short passage.

Breathing is movement which can be clearly (and deliciously) felt. Free breathing is beautiful to feel and beautiful to see. (p. 73)

—Barbara Conable
in *How to Learn the
Alexander Technique*

What do you want to say? You've left a whole page of poetry but no place to take a breath. (p. 58)

—Bernard Greenhouse
in Diane Asséo Griliches,
Teaching Musicians

We are at liberty to be real, or to be unreal. We may be true or false, the choice is ours. We may now wear one mask and now another, and never, if we so desire, appear with our own true face. But we cannot make these choices with impunity. Causes have effects, and if we lie to ourselves and to others, then we cannot expect to find truth and reality whenever we happen to want them. If we have chosen the way of falsity, we must not be surprised that truth eludes us when we finally come to need it. (p. 214)

—Thomas Merton
in Richard Todd,
The Thing Itself

Trust thyself. Every heart vibrates to that iron string. Envy is ignorance...Imitation is suicide. (p. 228)

—Ralph Waldo Emerson
in Richard Todd,
The Thing Itself

All conductors and performers have moments of pristine clarity in their thought processes, but these moments generally pass us by because we are not aware that they happen. They are short quiet times that coincide with our inhalation process. The poet John Audelay in the twelfth century referred to such processes as moments that "bind blood to bone." Breath in those moments binds human emotion to expressive thought. This binding process is the heart of this book. It is an awareness of the power of the specific time in the chain of events characterized by the creative process within the artist's soul. It is a moment of quiet solitude, intense clarity of idea, and the human will for the breath to be the carrier of that idea.

If you allow and accept that there is a clairvoyant "opening at the moment of inhalation," then you can feel a certain freedom to empower the breath with its message. Music teachers often say that musicians must "go deeper," but that eludes the real process involved within the performer. "Going deeper" is a separate process and a separate path, and that journey is one that must be taken separately. According to William Sloan Coffin, it is the "journey from the head to the heart." "Going deeper" is a label for that intensely personal journey every musician must ultimately take to empower the breath. This knowledge is not automatic, and in many ways it only becomes known at an intuitive level after one acknowledges that it does indeed exist. "Going deeper" must be known to each person in a very personal way. Perhaps the most accurate definition of one's center is where one lives deep within oneself. Knowledge of self is acquired through acknowledgment that it does in fact exist, and that one has mined sufficiently within oneself to find it.

Also prerequisite to breath empowerment is the belief that one has a message that can be relayed through the composer's craft.

THE MOMENT OF SILENCE

Psychologists explain that when artists are confronted with any decision about either their living or musicing, after processing ideas and thoughts, there is a silent nanosecond within the brain where a "decision" is made. That nanosecond of silence, for an artist, is the moment at which the musical and human idea is clarified and becomes crystal clear. For conductors, that moment must correspond with the breath. In many of us, however, the idea comes after the breath, during the actual performance of a musical phrase, which sabotages musical and human expression at every turn.

In that moment when a nanosecond of silence is the byproduct of thought, it is in *that* moment when we must bind that idea, that truth, that artistic honesty to our breath. In that moment, our breath becomes the messenger that informs our tone and all we create in our world of sound. That moment of the binding of breath to idea must be sacred in our creative process. With every breath comes another "moment" to bind human message to the composer's score. This process, above all, is a process of acknowledgment of the power of that nanosecond to provide truth and honest artistic expression in our music making. It is at the moment of inhalation that our truths about the music are powerfully bonded together. The idea is created with the breath, not as we are in the process of creating sounds or influencing them through conducting gesture. Musical idea is forethought rather than afterthought. Breath carries the musical forethought, which is the truth and the idea that is messaged through either text, notes, or both.

CHAPTER 4

INTENTION AND REVELATION

The relation of the performer to the composition that he is recreating is therefore a delicate one. When the interpreter injects his personality into a performance to an unwarranted degree, misunderstandings arise. (p. 225)

—Aaron Copland
in *What to Listen for in Music*

As poets and painters of centuries have tried to tell us, art is not about the expression of talent or the making of pretty things. It is about the preservation and containment of soul. It is about arresting life and making it available for contemplation. Art captures the eternal in the everyday, and it is the eternal that feeds soul—the whole world in a grain of sand. (p. 303)

—Thomas Moore
in *Care of the Soul*

Art is simply a result of expression during right feeling...Any
material will do. After all, the object is not to make art, but to
be in the wonderful state which makes art inevitable. (p. 45)

—Robert Henri
from *The Art Spirit*
in *Art as a Way of Life*

The relationships between performers and their instruments
and performers and their audiences can create a dilemma.
This aspect of a performer's presence in front of their audience
is often neglected in lessons due to emphasis on what is
perceived to be basic technique. What I have found is that
unless the lesson includes work on presence, as much as 40
percent of tone quality can be missing. (p. 848)

The first prerequisite for presence in performance is
focusing on the musical message rather than yourself. Often I
have to remind students that the message is far more important
than the performer. The passion and enthusiasm of the music
must be fueled by a genuine desire of the performer to be
there. (p. 851)

—Maribeth Bunch
from "Are You All
There" in *Strad*

The condition of being human can obviously be as large or as
small as the human being chooses it to be... (p. 11)

—Daniel Barenboim
in *Music Quickens Time*

When imagination is allowed to move to deep places, the sacred is revealed. The more different kinds of thoughts we experience around a thing and the deeper our reflections go as we are arrested by its artfulness, the more fully its sacredness can emerge. (p. 289)

As the poets and painters of centuries have tried to tell us, art is not about the expression of talent or the making of pretty things. It is about the preservation and containment of soul. It is about arresting life and making it available for contemplation. (p. 303)

"Soul" is not a thing, but a quality or a dimension of experiencing life and ourselves. It has to do with depth, value, relatedness, heart, and personal substance. (p. 5)

Observance of the soul can be deceptively simple. You take back what has been disowned. You work with what is, rather than with what you wish were there. (p. 9)

—Thomas Moore
in *Care of the Soul*

Authenticity may seem bold, for it's often original, one of a kind. Separate from consensus. One comes to it through trust in one's own self, and a willingness to entrust oneself to others, whatever the risk. Vulnerability at some point dissolves into stillness. This stillness can act, and does act, for children and the child in oneself, as a kind of buffer, an insulating protection, which allows one to be authentic and at risk in a natural way. (p. 120)

—M. C. Richards
in *Opening Our
Moral Eye*

The plant has two forces. The part that goes up into the light
and the force that goes into the dark, into the earth. There is
a place in some plants that is only one cell wide called "the
crossing point"—where those two impulses co-exist. This is
where our wholeness is.

—M. C. Richards
in *The Fire Within*

For the breath to provide an immediate clairvoyance into the sound
that grows out of a breath, it seems that the breath must be empowered
with a clear human and musical *intention*. If you ponder the process
before you speak, what you will say and how you will say it is decided
at the moment you inhale! You do not decide what you are going to
say once you begin to speak. Aside from allowing your body to breathe,
you must have a deep, profound, and intuitive belief that your breath
can indeed carry a message—and that message comes at the moment of
inhalation, or inspiration.

MUSICAL WILL OR MUSICAL INTENTION?

Musicians often confuse musical will and musical intention. If one
wills a musical idea into the musicing process, and then constantly
exerts that will while the music is being created, then there is a certain
amount of stifling control that enters into the music making. Especially
with conductors, who influence others in the musicing process, musical
will in and of itself can be a dangerous and often lethal ingredient if not
mixed with other human aspects.

Intention seems to imply forethought rather than afterthought in the musicing. The intention contained within the breath can be powerful and compelling. Intentional breathing implies there is a process by which intention is arrived at. For musicians, there is a seven-step psychological/awareness process (described on the pages that follow) to enable them to infuse intention into the breath:

1. Stillness (life)
2. Opening yourself and your body
3. Being at center and going into the crossing point
4. Intention
5. Breathing into the intention (idea)
6. Allowing others to read the breath
7. Releasing unencumbered sound

For the breath to have intention, this sequential process allows you to examine yourself prior to the inhalation and after the point of inhalation to reveal that breathing alone might be insufficient, and that contained within the word *breath* is a wonderful sequence of events that allows you to fully realize the communicative power within each breath.

1. STILLNESS (LIFE)

Stillness mortifies the outward senses and resurrects the inward movements, whereas an outward manner of life does the opposite, that is, it resurrects the outward senses and deadens the inward movements. (p. 175)

—Saint Isaac the Syrian
from *The Ascetical Homilies*

For many, the initial step in this sequence will be the major challenge. There is a calm within stillness that allows you to be aware that you are about to breathe. That awareness grants musicians the freedom to breathe deeply; it enables them to allow air to enter into their body in a natural way.

Stillness is important because it not only allows you to begin the breathing process, but it is within stillness that idea, or intention, is born.

2. OPENING YOURSELF AND YOUR BODY

This is the part of the psychological breath process that can only be realized if you are vulnerable to some degree. There is something about vulnerability that allows breath to take on an honest and authentic role in what you are about to do. Breath taken without vulnerability will be devoid of its power to be the connective tissue between idea and expression.

Vulnerability has a certain feeling within you. When you are vulnerable, you are very aware of your internal space.[3] Vulnerability is also immediately perceived by others. Conversely, an absence of vulnerability is also immediately perceived, and prohibits or impedes any further honest human connection from occurring. *Its presence in this process is everything.* Perhaps it is part of our human nature, but many of us will do anything to avoid being vulnerable. Vulnerablity is perceived as a point of weakness rather than strength. (This is addressed in more detail in the next chapter.)

---

3   My favorite discussion on vulnerability is in *The Musician's Soul* (1999).

3. BEING AT CENTER AND GOING INTO THE CROSSING POINT

In *Toward Center* (2009), I presented the idea that one's center is the place from which one's need to connect with others (to extend outward from within) coexists with one's need to be rooted and grounded. Both of these powerful human forces cohabitate in a specific point that is located in our anatomical "center," which is also the place where all that we believe lives within us. You must have both for human ideas to be shared with others—idea, or intention, is birthed in this place.

4. INTENTION

I was having a discussion about this book with one of my former students who is studying martial arts. She spoke passionately about what she is learning—above all, that every gesture must have a clear and direct intention! While the word *idea* is a strong word, the word *intention* seems to carry both the meaning behind the word idea and a stronger, more direct course of action for us as artists.

Artistry is born when a conductor's musical idea moves beyond thought or musical analysis and becomes an intention. The best-rehearsed passages will remain just that, well-rehearsed passages, if at some point the conductor does not fill that structure of clarified pitch and rhythm with idea and intention. A conductor's rehearsal procedure is layered with many ideas, but it is the overriding intention that gives the ideas meaning in sound.

5. BREATHING INTO THE INTENTION (IDEA)

Once you decide what is to be said musically, then you need to breathe into that intention. Period. Don't just breathe; *breathe into the intentional idea*. Always strive for breath with intention. If you believe breath can carry intention, then it will do just that. It will be extremely difficult for your musicing to carry any compelling and *clear* message without an intentional breath that carries the idea. Clear, honest, and direct communication, I am sure you would agree, is the goal. But without intentional breath, your communication may be clouded, elusive, and even difficult to hear or feel as others listen to your music.

6. ALLOWING OTHERS TO READ THE BREATH

When conducting, at the moment air enters your body, the body physically opens. Air falls into your nose and mouth. Your mouth is a strong indicator to your ensemble of your openness and vulnerability. A closed mouth denotes, subconsciously, that you are not breathing, you are not open and vulnerable, or both.

Physical opening not only invites a reaction to your breath, but it also immediately communicates a vulnerability that allows the idea (intention) to take flight! Your face is a mirror of what is happening deep within you. When you hug someone, the most powerful part of the embrace is not the strength of the embrace, but the air going out of your body as you embrace. It is your opening that allows your released air to carry your care or your love. This, the most basic element of human communication, is the same physical and spiritual act you must transcribe directly to your music-making process. Your music-making breathing must become organic and human in the same way that your human embrace does. From birth, human beings are able to communicate through embrace and breath deep human feelings and experiences. You need only apply this most basic element of communication to how you breathe as a musician.

7. RELEASING UNENCUMBERED SOUND

Musicians often feel like they must move as they perform. Certainly for some musicians, without movement, instruments make no sound (e.g., keys must be depressed and resonators must vibrate to make sound). However, movement that does not directly relate to the production of sound sometimes wears the disguise of communicating musicianship and musical idea—and at times actually interferes with both the production of the sound and the musical idea.

If you breathe into the idea, then all you need to do is release the sound. For many years I thought that sound is being created and I should influence that sound as it was being produced. But I have learned that we should no more interrupt this miracle of creation than we interrupt our speech once it has begun. Extraneous movement while singing or playing, nonessential gesture when conducting, robs an idea (if there is one) of its potency. The sound produced should deliver the idea. Personal *external* kinesthetic will always mask honest and direct human expression.

As a conductor, you must believe in the power of the breath for it to assume its very compelling role in the musicing process. Sound should be borne out of intentional breath. To paraphrase Descartes:

I breathe, therefore, I am.

CHAPTER 5

Breathing into the Vulnerable Opening that Is the Soul

But when this beauty and brightness has filled the inmost part of the heart, it must become outwardly visible, and not be like a lamp hidden under a bushel, but be a light shining in the darkness, which cannot be hidden. It shines out, and by the brightness of its rays it makes the body a mirror of the mind, spreading through the limbs and senses so that every action, every word, look, movement and even laugh (if there should be laughter) radiates gravity and honor. (p. 29)

—St. Bernard
in Rembert Herbert,
*Entrances: Gregorian
Chant in Daily Life*

Only he who himself turns to the other human being and opens himself to him receives the world in him. Only the being whose otherness, accepted by my being, lives and faces me in the whole compression of existence, brings the radiance of eternity to me. Only when two say to one another with all that they are, "It is Thou," is the indwelling of the Present Being between them. (p. 35)

—Martin Buber
in *Between Man
and Man*

The soul is generous: it takes in the needs of the world. The soul is wise: it suffers without shutting down. The soul is hopeful: it engages the world in ways that keep opening our hearts. The soul is creative: it finds a path between realities that might defeat us and fantasies that are mere escapes. All we need to do is to bring down the wall that separates us from our own souls and deprives the world of the soul's regenerative powers. (p. 184)

—Parker Palmer
in *A Hidden Wholeness*

In the final analysis, we count for something only because of the essential we embody, and if we do not embody that, life is wasted. (p. x)

—C. G. Jung
in James Hillman,
The Soul's Code

It may be more important to be awake than to be successful, balanced, or healthy. What does it mean to be awake? Perhaps to be living with a lively imagination, responding honestly and courageously to opportunity and avoiding the temptation to follow mere habit or collective values. It means to be an individual, in every instance manifesting the originality of who we are. This is the ultimate form of creativity—following the lead of the deep soul as we make a life.

We all fall asleep and allow life to rush by without reflection and consideration. When we are shocked into awareness by tragedy or failure, this is the time not simply to make resolutions for the future, but to choose to live an awakened life. The Buddha was called "the awakened one." (pp. 126–127)

—Thomas Moore
in *Original Self*

Man sees the things that surround him long before he becomes aware of his own self. Many of us are conscious of the hiddenness of things, but few of us sense the mystery of our own presence. (p. 61)

—Abraham Joshua Heschel
in *Between God and Man*

The soul gives life and sensation to the body: There are two kinds of living beings, those which have sensation and those which do not. The sensate rank above the insensate, and above both them is life, by which one lives and senses. Life and living do not rank equally, much less life and lifelessness. Life is the living soul, but it does not derive its life from any other source than itself; strictly speaking, we describe this as life rather than living. When it is infused into the body it gives life, so that the body, through the presence of life, becomes life but living. From this it is clear that, even for a living body, to be is not the same as to live, since it can be but not be alive. (pp. 7–8)

—St Bernard of Clairvaux
in John R. Sommerfeldt,
*The Spiritual Teachings
of Bernard of Clairvaux*

Over the years, my students have often remarked that breathing is difficult in the context of music performance; they have difficulty "breathing." It is not the breath that is the challenge, but the *opening of oneself* that must occur before the breath falls into the body. Opening is the real issue. The moment before breath is taken must be a moment of incredible and profoundly deep vulnerability if the breath is to be empowered with musical and human message. It is not the breath but the opening that determines both the quality and honesty of the breath's message.

To understand the power of that moment immediately before inhalation is somewhat elusive. Most assume that breathing is such a natural process that all one must do is simply take a breath. The challenge here is that you are not simply taking a breath in the biological, life-maintaining sense. Instead, you are using your breath to carry a message: to transport not only a musical idea, but also human emotional ideas. The challenge is to open yourself to allow the message to be carried on the breath at inhalation.

The opening of the body is not an easy task. First, it takes a will to empower the breath. Second, you must leave issues of life clutter at the rehearsal room or stage door. You must be in a state that allows you to let go—to allow an opening of your body that creates a great internal space which the air then occupies, borne with musical intent. This is an intentional process that makes you acutely aware of every cubic centimeter of breath that enters into your body. During that opening, you make a conscious choice to infuse the air with your message, with the musical idea. Inhalation is preceded by inspiration that comes at the moment of opening the body.

To further comprehend this paradigm, you must surrender the old idea that musical phrase is created as the phrase is being sounded. This approach to musicianship results in a manipulation of phrase, a forced trajectory that is usually never compelling to the listeners and whose sheer dynamic is incapable of bearing idea. A sung or a played phrase *is* the embodiment of a breath first inspired during opening and then inhaled.

THE AUDIATIONAL BREATH

In addition to the breath transporting the musical idea, there is another equally important part of that opening of the body. At the same time the idea is birthed in the opening of the body, one's audiation is activated. Edwin E. Gordon has long advocated breath before musical performance because the breath also carries within it the audiation of what is to follow (discussed further in Chapter 9). The music, in fact, is heard before it is ever sounded physically, in all its dimensions. Its pitch, rhythm, dynamic, and style are all audiated simultaneously at the moment, which psychologists have labeled as the "moment of choice." This moment of inspiration before exhalation is the most powerful thing we can do as conductors and musicians. Its effect is immediately profound, and immediately sensed and perceived.

The inhalation process described here immediately begins both the transport of human idea and musical intent. Breath is simply the most compelling thing you can do as a musician. Its mastery is not a choice; rather, it is your obligation as an artist to master and understand all of the components and miracles the breath can birth, communicate, and relay. Breathing with intention must become a commitment that is central to one's artistry. Breath's power over the musical birthing process humanizes expression and infuses honesty into sound. It is that honesty in the sound that connects performers to each other and connects performers to listeners. And of equal importance, the inspired breath in all its dimensions connects each of us to the composer's message in the most intimate of ways. Whether we realize it or not, this musical intimacy is what we all deeply yearn for as musicians.

So what are the consequences of not giving breath its due? I have heard many ensembles that sing impeccably without empowerment of breath. They are in tune, and their tone has a particular aesthetic, but because the tone is born out of a breath process that is either non-existent or malnourished, it is unable to carry human idea in such a way that is both compelling and profound. This difficult conundrum is usually set in motion by a conductor who does not breathe, or an accompanist who does not breathe. The ensemble will breathe whether or not the person at the front of the room is breathing. But without the conductor inspiriting the musical idea into the breath before inhalation, the musical idea is manipulated into the phrase by external means rather than being borne in the breath.

You must profoundly believe in the spiritual power of the breath opening/inspiration/inhalation process. Like any skill or technique, it must be developed out of a will to empower breath with something on a higher plane than just taking in air. Breath is the most powerful vehicle for the birthing and transport of musical idea and musical intent. Think of breath as the reactor that creates the musical reaction that will follow it in sound!

You must also possess a bit of humbleness to understand that breath is a miracle that cannot be explained. While I attempt to analyze the components to create an empowered breath, the magic it creates in the music that follows cannot be explained. It simply happens. Musical magic is what we all want. And you will come a bit closer to creating that magic if you ponder the miracles and mysteries that breath carries within it.

CHAPTER 6

UNDERSTANDING THE MECHANICS OF BREATHING THROUGH SOMATICS: HOW DOES BREATH COME INTO THE BODY?

Most people assume that breathing comes and remains a natural part of living. They take for granted that the rate of breathing will alter and its rhythmic pattern change and the demands of the blood stream and so on change. Awareness of the rhythm and pattern of breathing, Laban wrote in his first book, is important simply because drawing in the breath of life is central to so much of our activity. Understanding the ribcage and its points of expansion, together with some training in the more expansive use of the lower chest, can aid individual oxygen supply and control as well as its economy of use. Breathing is central to the demands of effort and recovery, for unnecessary tension created by the ineffectual use of breathing often occurs because of disharmonic inner states of mind. (p. 60)

—John Hodgson and
Valerie Preston-Dunlop
in *Rudolf Laban: An
Introduction to His
Work and Influence*

Author's Note:

In writing this book, I was blessed with the good fortune of coming across a supplemental resource that I feel is necessary to understand the breath process— bringing oneself into awareness of one's breathing processes through somatics and Body Mapping. I must give a great deal of credit to Barbara Conable; her teaching changed the path of my own teaching and my understanding of the architecture and function of the body in conducting and, more importantly, breath. In this chapter, I set out to explain the principles involved with the physical act of breathing to begin the awareness process. However, you would certainly clarify and reinforce your understanding of this information by viewing the DVD Move Well, Avoid Injury *(GIA, 2010) by Barbara Conable and Amy Likar. In addition, there is a companion DVD to this book, which presents Yoga as a way to identify and heighten your awareness as to what parts of your body are carrying tension and locking the free inhalation and exhalation process. By practicing Yoga, you learn to still your mind while being aware of your body. It is a means by which you can sensitize yourself to the inhalation and exhalation of breath.*

For musicians, breathing directly influences tempo, tone color, shape of phrase, dynamic, and spiritual content of the tone. For the conductor, the breath not only affects the tone of the singer, but the conductor's exhalation profoundly affects the human content of the tone. All of these factors that involve the breath are the wild cards, so to speak, in any rehearsal or performance. A conductor or performer who gains understanding of the breath and its impact upon the sound will gain one of the most valuable rehearsal and performance tools. This book is not a technical manual on the mechanics of breathing; it is intended to provide clearer paradigms for allowing breath to enter the body. The Yogic approach to accessing breath, as presented by Mark Moliterno later in this book and on the companion DVD, demonstrates how to access breath and self-educate yourself on where your breath may be held or restricted as you breathe. *The Yoga exercises advocated in this book teach access, not use.* Breathing for singing or playing is task specific, and that art should be respected. Yoga enables you to realize what restricts you from breathing.

Quite simply, if a musician is to breathe, then the conductor must also breathe. The breath of a musician can be influenced by a conductor. The conductor must prepare every entrance through a breath that is imbued with human content. A musician must do likewise.

Breathing is a two-step process. First, you must be able to open your body to prepare for the breath to enter your body. This is perhaps the most difficult aspect of the act of inhalation. Many conductors confuse opening the body and inhalation, and combine both of the steps. The resultant breath is what I call a "Muppet" breath. The mouth opens, but air doesn't really enter the body, nor does it fall into a deep-seated location within the body. This breath is characterized by the mouth opening at the moment of inhalation.

If the breath is properly taken, your mouth will open as a part of the breath preparation process. When inhalation is activated by the physical process of breathing, then air will simply and gently fall into the body. When done in this manner, the choir will breathe at the same moment, almost by instinct. These moments of breath should be the most magical points of any rehearsal or performance.

EIGHT-HANDED BREATHING: UNDERSTANDING INHALATION AND EXHALATION

The major factor that impedes proper inhalation and exhalation in both conductors and singers is a misconception as to how the breath works in an anatomical sense. Consider the eight-handed breathing technique presented on the pages that follow.[4]

When breath enters the body, what part of the body moves first, second, third, and fourth? If the conductor or the choir do not understand this process, then unfortunately neither the conductor or the choir will breathe well, and the tone of the choir will be adversely affected.

---

4   A video version of eight-handed breathing to show to choirs, or for conductor's study and understanding, can be found on the *Evoking Sound: Body Mapping Principles and Basic Conducting Technique* DVD (GIA, 2002).

THE BODY MECHANICS OF BREATHING

The following parts of the body move in succession when inhalation occurs:

THE INHALATION PROCESS

1. **Ribs** of the back traverse or travel outward, with each rib traveling at its own rate.

2. The **Diaphragm** moves from a more domed to a less domed position.

3. The **Abdominal Walls** (front and sides) move outward.

4. The **Pelvic Floor** drops slightly.

Note: Inhalation *always* occurs in this order, with all of the parts always participating!

The following parts of the body move in succession when exhalation occurs:

THE EXHALATION PROCESS

1. **Ribs** of the back traverse or travel inward, with each rib traveling at its own rate.

2. The **Diaphragm** moves from a less domed to a more domed position.

3. The **Abdominal Walls** (front and sides) move inward.

4. The **Pelvic Floor** raises slightly.

Note: It is important to understand that the order of movement of the anatomy of the body is the same for exhalation as it is for inhalation! Many conductors and singers believe that, anatomically, the exhalation process is the reverse of the inhalation process. This is a perceptual fantasy! Correction of this misnomer will dramatically improve the tone and expressivity of any ensemble.

The movement of breathing is sequential, and it is also unified, or coordinated, in a way that makes it feel like a single movement top to bottom when we are free of tension. (p. 33)

—Barbara Conable
in *The Structures and
Movement of Breathing*

THE AWARENESS OF LENGTHENING AND GATHERING

There is an important awareness that must be in place for breath to "come into" the body. As you inhalate and exhale, there is a natural gathering of the spine on inhalation and a lengthening of the spine on exhalation. You must be aware of this anatomical truth for breath to come into your body. The awareness of both lengthening and gathering can help achieve a supple interior space for the breath. Remember, on inhalation the spine gathers, and on exhalation the spine lengthens. Use the following diagrams to accurately map your body as the air enters you like a wave.

gathering
of the spine

lengthening
of the spine

CHAPTER 7

BREATH DEFINES OUR INTERIORITY

We must understand that, in terms of the geography of the body, singing is profoundly interior. There is a wonderful convergence in the centrality or interiority or coreness of singing in our human body and our human spirit, since we experience singing coming from "deep within" emotionally and intellectually. Singing is deeply integrative of body and spirit in another way, as well. As singers achieve mastery, their conception of the music and their conception of the movement that manifests the music arise within them simultaneously. (p. 45)

> —Barbara Conable
> in *The Structures and*
> *Movement of Breathing*

If the human body, in relation to singing, is the vehicle both of art and life itself, then breathing fulfills a most important function because it sustains both life and song. All living and all singing is dependent upon breathing. The first sign of life in an infant is the presence of respiratory activity, and from that moment breathing holds all vocal utterance including singing, concomitantly to the course and stream of life. (p. 15)

Corporate (simultaneous) breathing is one of the essential means toward achieving a vital corporate unity within a choir. By inhaling together in the mood of the music, a psychological relationship is developed which welds individual singers together. (p. 24)

—Wilhelm Ehmann
in *Choral Directing*

It is commonly said that the ancient peoples of the north have many words to describe the subtleties of what we refer to merely as "snow," and that those of the forest have hundreds of words for shades of green. Anyone who meditates knows that the same might be said of the breath. Each breath moment is its own universe. In meditation, we come to know something about this terrain in ways that open doors, that bring us back to our senses, that refine our hearts, that help us understand what it means to be human, what it means to be whole, right here, right now. (p. xi)

—Larry Rosenberg
in *Breath by Breath*

When you argue, you cannot sing.
When you cling, you cannot move.
When you clench, you cannot breathe.
When you grasp, you cannot possess.
When you possess, you cannot savor.

> from "Twenty Three"
> in *The Tao of Musicianship*
> Gary Bede Camera, OSB

Essentially, mindfulness entails a new way of paying attention, a way to expand the scope of awareness while refining its precision. In this training of the mind we learn to let go of the thoughts and feelings that pull us out of the present moment, and to steady our awareness on our immediate experience. If distraction breeds emotional turmoil, the ability to sustain our gaze, to keep looking, can bring greater clarity and insight. (p. 9)

> —Tara Bennett-Goleman
> in *Emotional Alchemy*

The great poet Gerard Manley Hopkins created the word "inscape" to describe one's inner life—the part that defines you and gives meaning to your most profound human expression. That being said, you might do well to ponder how, when, and why that interior landscape is created within you and why you should cultivate its very shape and size, or why you should even be worried about it. You might even wonder whether you could indeed cultivate or create such an internal space.

Once cultivated, you might possibly ponder its affect on your expressive will.

The concept of internal spaciousness, at least an awareness of it, must be at the core of what we do as artists. For without *interiority,* human ideas manifest through the sounds we influence and make have no resonance in the real world. My students often accuse me (many times rightly so) of making up words, but this is not one of those times. The Oxford Compact Dictionary defines interiority as "the quality of being interior or inward." So the word does exist! The concept of interiority is seldom part of audible discussion among musicians.

The first step is acknowledgment that such a space exists within you. Once acknowledged, you can then begin to move things around within yourself to allow that space to happen. Interior space can be willed. Vulnerability creates the initial opening, but it is the breath that determines its depth and shape. By acknowledging the power of breath to hewn a place within you, you create a vesicle that is the primary vehicle for human emotion. There is a void within you that yearns to be filled...and that interior fulfillment is created by your inhalation. The exhalation is the communicative part of the breath process; the inhalation is the birthing part of the process. The concept seems so simple, yet it is hard to realize.

THE WANT TO BREATHE

The want to breathe is ultimately rooted in a want to share. Breath taken seems to have the tendency to want to be shared via exhalation. That is simple physics. But the ability to imbue that breath with human spirit is a willed event. The breath you take can be laden with life messages. To be sure, you must know the messages you want to transmit, and make no mistake about it, you can transmit powerful messages from the deep interiority of yourself.

I struggle so to convince my students of the power of breath, I think primarily because they have not spent enough time realizing and accepting at a basic level that they have interior space, and that space *is* their expressive apparatus. The realization that it is internal space which communicates marks the coming of age of any musician or artist. The human condition allows you this incredible vesicle for the birthing and growth of idea. In other words, your interior space is the place where wonder and awe hold fort within you.

The Birth of Internal Spaciousness: Childhood

If we think back to our childhood, to what it felt like to be a child, internal spaciousness was a constant back then. Our bodies felt buoyant because of the vastness of our interior space. Creatively, we knew no fear, and we expressed ourselves honestly and directly in all we did. Whether it was moving, singing, or the endless artwork we drew, all of it came from this vastness within us. Breath was a part of that process: we took in vast amounts and used it just as quickly for the purpose of self-expression. Then somewhere along the way, for some reason, we began to close. Our interior space became smaller, we relied on outside expressive devices, and as a result our breath became smaller because we lost our interior life.

So now I am proposing a type of reclamation for you. First, reclaim what is rightfully yours, your interior space. Then work to fill it with breath. Once the breath begins again to enter you in a way that breeds interior space, then its exhalation can carry ideas once again. Breath and its power must become a passionate force within you; you must want the breath to carry the message within you. Acknowledgment that breath can do this is the first step toward a long trajectory of expressive growth and artistic honesty. You can will the breath to carry these messages into your musicing if you believe it to be so. The breath can create a space in which beauty, awe, and wonder can reside in you. An appreciation that you have such an internal space will be sufficient to allow a place for breath to fall into!

> An appreciation for beauty is simply an openness to the power of things to stir the soul. If you can be affected by beauty, then soul is alive and well in us, because the soul's great talent is for being affected. The word passion means basically 'to be affected,' and passion is the essential energy of the soul. The poet Rilke describes this passive power in the imagery of the flower's structure, when he calls it a 'muscle of infinite reception.' We don't often think of the capacity to be affected as strength and as the work of a powerful muscle, and yet for the soul, as for the flower, this is its toughest work and its main role in our lives. (p. 280)

> —Thomas Moore
> in *Care of the Soul*

CHAPTER 8

THE IDEA INFORMS THE BODY

Absolute truth. Take a breath that is already the thought.

> —Thomas Hampson
> Master class at
> Westminster Choir
> College
> November 19, 2009

The impulse behind the creation of music is not expressional in the Western psychological sense but is brought into existence by a dynamic process which is inclusive rather than exclusive; which, so to speak, is natural rather than rational. (p. 159)

> —Jamake Highwater
> in *The Primal Mind*

All living creatures possess this function of timing, whose purpose it is to integrate the three dimensions of somatic being into effective actions. Only one creature, the human being, possesses a sensory awareness that can be directed away from the external world and focused inwardly on the internal functioning of our somatic process. When this sensory awareness is directed inward to the undeveloped or atrophied processes of our living bodies, these processes change—and they change for the better, because more has been integrated into the ongoing process of our lives. In brief, we become more adaptable by integrating new fragments into the whole process of our central nervous system. The total somatic process is thereby improved: Our actions improve, our balance improves, our thinking improves, our judgment improves, our emotional tone improves—in short, our lives improve. (p. 123)

—Thomas Hanna
in *The Body of Life*

Mental activity tends to become conscious when reflection and deliberation are involved in the completion of the response pattern, that is, when automatic behavior is disturbed because a tendency has been inhibited. (p. 31)

—Leonard Meyer
in *Emotion and Meaning
in Music*

Humility in the artist is his frank acceptance of all experiences, just as Love in the artist is simply that sense of Beauty that reveals to the world its body and its soul. (p. 265)

> —Oscar Wilde
> in Thomas Moore,
> *Care of the Soul*

Life knocks the corners off; age, or experience, accounts for some degree of transformation in every artist. "One hears new implications," he said. "I think one has a tendency to take more time. One listens and takes time to listen. One is not afraid to more deeply characterize certain ideas."

The silences are particularly striking. Mr. Fleisher tells his students that "silence is not the absence of music" and urges them to play, judiciously, "as late as possible, without being late." Among the most surprising effects on his recent recordings are heart-stopping moments of anticipation, distending time as the listener waits for a note that begins to seem as if it will never come. "It's almost an instant of panic: Where is it?" Mr. Fleisher acknowledged. "We're talking about nanoseconds."

> —Leon Fleisher
> in "A Pianist for Whom
> Never Was Never an
> Option"
> *The New York Times*
> June 10, 2007

THE POWER WITHIN THE REST

Most musicians, especially conductors, have not spent enough time understanding the power within the seemingly simple act of inhaling and exhaling: a breath. This miraculous act is assigned two specific locales in our musicing: (1) before a work begins or is birthed, and (2) within the confines of those miracle moments within any musical composition: the rest.

Rests are frequently overlooked with regard to their mystical powers to influence the trajectory of phrases. They are viewed as necessary points in the music, points of repose and restart. But buried deep within those "vacancies" of active sound are profound moments of opportunity for both musical idea and human connection. We have all acknowledged in passing that rests are a part of the musical idea, yet they are given only fleeting attention. Because they are silent, rests tend not to attract attention. Perhaps you should readjust your musicing psyche. Recreate the importance of a rest in your mind as not just an opportunity for the infusion of musical idea and musical thought, but as THE miraculous opportunity to infuse both the expressive idea in effect and color, and the human content that is to be carried in any musical phrase.

Whether or not it's true, I want to believe that in some way composers deeply ponder placement of rests. Whether they do so consciously or not, if the compositional process has an organic nature at its root, then how their music "breathes" is part of the architectural structure of their conception. I find it fascinating to consider the placement of rests, especially when a work changes idea. In fact, as a conductor, I have tended on first study of a score to look for rests and their role in clarifying and illuminating the phrase structure—that is, in the case of choral music, whether they connect text ideas or are used to change emotional and expressive direction within the piece.

RESTS AS RESPITES: THE CLAIRVOYANT OPPORTUNITY

Rests must be viewed as *clairvoyant opportunities*. They must be viewed as the only opportunities for both performers and conductor to birth and re-birth awe and wonder into the sounds being sung or played through the inhalation. Every inhalation provides the profoundly human chance to make your thoughts audible. Making musical ideas live in sound can only happen in the opportunity provided by rests. To be able to open your body and at the very same moment empower the breath with your musical and human ideas about phrase, all bound into one inhalation, is a vital part of everything you do as an artist. Perceived in this way, rests filled with meaningful inhalation will not only infuse your musicing with meaningfulness but also, at times, be redemptive in a musicing process or performance gone awry.

Rests should never be ignored, yet we all do it. We do not mean to do it, but somehow we get all wrapped up in the technical aspects of the music we create. When we think of all of the details we must deal with to make the music right, we tend to discount or ignore the breath because it is silent! Instead, learn to take care of *all* of the details of your musicing, including the breath. If you believe there is a certain mysticism in what you do, then you must consider the possibilities carried within the inhalation.

BREATHING INTO THE IDEA:
THE MUSICIAN'S DEEPEST CHALLENGE

Breathe into the idea. Sounds simple enough. But while it may sound simple, it holds the key to artistry and musicianship for all: what you breathe "into" is as important as the idea you breathe. While we can all grasp the concept of a musical idea, what is elusive is the open space that this idea is deposited into at the moment of inhalation. The power of the idea has everything to do with the openness of that space. It is the spaciousness that allows air to fall into the body; it is also the space that serves as the home for musical and human ideas.

That being said, you must next consider how you are able to acquire that space for the idea just before breathing into the idea. That moment of profound opening is the challenge. For if your idea is to be honest, then the space that houses it must also be honest. Thought of in another way, the space that you breathe into is your most soulful place. Your interior space is your very soul. The map of your internal space can be thought of as soul. *It is not just something we breathe into; we breathe into ourselves.* Your art must be part of your life, and perhaps a part of your way of living and being with others. Thomas Moore, in *Care of the Soul*, talks about acquiring this sacred space more succinctly than I could ever hope to define this open place that is so necessary for our understanding of breath:

> Living artfully, therefore, might require something as simple as *pausing*. Some people are incapable of being arrested by things because they are always on the move. A common symptom of modern life is that there is no time for thought, or even for letting impressions of the day

sink in. Yet it is only when the world enters the heart that it can be made into soul. The vessel in which soul-making takes place is an inner container scooped out by reflection and wonder. There is no doubt that some people could spare themselves the expense and trouble of psychotherapy simply by giving themselves a few minutes each day for quiet reflection. This simple act would provide what is missing in their lives: a period of non-doing that is essential to the nourishment of the soul.

Akin to pausing, and just as important in care of the soul, is *taking time*. I realize these are extremely simple suggestions, but taken to heart they could transform a life, by allowing soul to enter. (pp. 286–287)

—Thomas Moore
in *Care of the Soul*

Amen. Enough said?

CHAPTER 9

THE AUDIATIONAL BREATH

Sound itself is not music. Sound becomes music through audiation, when, as with language, you translate sounds in your mind and give them meaning. The meaning you give to these sounds will be different depending on the occasion and will be different from the meaning given them by any other person. Audiation is the process of assimilating and comprehending (not simply rehearing) music we have just heard performed or have heard performed sometime in the past. We also audiate when we assimilate and comprehend in our minds music we may or may not have heard, but are reading in notation or composing or improvising. In contrast, aural perception takes place when we are actually hearing sound the moment it is being produced. We audiate actual sound only after we have aurally perceived it. In aural perception we are dealing with immediate sound events, whereas in audiation, we are dealing with delayed musical events. (pp. 3–4)

Through the process of audiation, we sing and move in our minds, without needing to sing and move physically. (p. 6)

It is also of utmost importance that a deep breath be taken by the teacher and students before a tonal pattern or rhythm pattern is performed. During inhalation, the pattern or patterns to be performed will naturally be prepared in the same way words are prepared in inhalation before speaking. Preparation assists students in learning to cross the bridge from sole imitation to both imitation and audiation by allowing them to hear silently and understand, as they inhale, what they are going to perform before they perform it. (p. 105)

—Edwin E. Gordon
in *Learning Sequences*
in Music (2007 Edition)

What is meant to be heard in music must be heard within you before anyone can hear it. (p. 70)

—Nadia Boulanger
in *Master Teacher*

Author's Note:

Earlier in this book I mentioned the concept of "audiational breath." Before I begin in this chapter to provide you with the background for my thought on this concept, I must be very clear that the concept of the audiational breath carrying musical information was first discussed and described by music psychologist Edwin Gordon, with whom I did my doctoral study. Were it not for his teaching and the wisdom he imparted to this naive student years ago, I would not have had the inspiration of his ideas, his teaching, and his insistence on mastering the art of sharing one's ideas through written and spoken word to write this book today. I also want to be very clear that I am not trying to interpret Dr. Gordon's concepts from the viewpoint of the performer and conductor, from my own experience and vantage point, or from the viewpoint of other performers who hold the same opinions as I do. My intent is to make a compelling argument as to the importance of breath for all we do musically, and help you realize how severely handicapped any musician is who does not empower breath and use breath to carry the human messages in musicing, and I believe that the foundation for such understanding is to understand and embrace Dr. Gordon's concept of audiation.

I also encourage you to reference the books on audiation listed in the bibliography of this book. While many teachings of Dr. Gordon have profoundly changed how we teach and learn music, perhaps no concept in the history of music education has held so much promise and responsibility as the concept of audiation. The teaching of audiation should be the overriding objective for all of us who teach and conduct. For without the power of audiation, our musicing is contrived, at times wooden, and many times dishonest. And without breath, whatever our message is, becomes muted, veiled, and vague.

WHAT IS AUDIATION AND WHAT IS ITS POWER?

Audiation, a coined term by Edwin Gordon, is all the things this book has discussed thus far. Gordon has defined audiation as the presence of sound when it is not physically present. For years he has drawn our pedagogical attention to the depth of audiation and its role in our musical development, creation, and performance. In the Glossary of the 2007 edition of *Learning Sequences in Music*, Gordon defines audiation as:

> Hearing and comprehending in one's mind the sound
> of music that is not, or may never have been, physically
> present. It is not imitation or memorization. There are
> six stages of audiation and eight types of audiation.
> (p. 399)

In this definition, Gordon identifies six stages and eight types of audiation. These types and stages clearly identify specific sub-processes that contribute to audiation. For the purposes of this book, I am trying to establish your belief in audiation, and that what is audiated can be carried into the sounds you make and can also transmit in the most direct and powerful ways musical and human information to your ensemble.

What is essential to all music making and conducting is a profound belief that the breath, and the breath alone, initiates all things musical and human in any act of musical creation. This belief must be so deep, so committed, that it is the basis of all that you do. It is the breath that is born out of audiation that empowers musicing beyond your wildest dreams, or even imagination. Understanding that audiation can carry not only specific music content (e.g., pitch, rhythm, tone color, tempo, articulation) but also human messages is the most powerful tool we have as musicians. Despite those aspects, we do not by and large teach audiation that is married intimately to every breath we take as performers and conductors. As a conductor, you must understand that if you do not breathe with audiational intent, then you sabotage all honest musical expression in your ensembles. While this statement may sound severe, it is true. Music is a series of action/reaction events. Without the action, there can be only limited reaction. And that action can only be set in motion by breath. For conductors, gesture can support musical ideas, but those ideas can be more efficiently birthed though breath.

Conductors cannot do without "expressive" conducting technique. It is vital to understand the very intimate relationship of gesture to sound—that is, conducting technique that mirrors and assists the musicing process. But you also must force yourself into an awareness that it is breath born out of your clairvoyant audiation that is the igniting fuse for music making. This will require a giving of yourself to breath and its power. It is the most difficult of challenges. Believing that breath can be so powerful requires a new awareness of breath and how you breathe, and it requires you to assign to the breath some of the things you have thought were heretofore carried within your conducting technique. Technique is the messenger, but it is the breath that gives both message and human purpose to what you do as a musician. That message and human purpose is born in audiation. You hear it before anyone else, and then you breathe *into* that audiation. When audiation followed by breath becomes your overriding musical purpose, then you will find that your music making, rehearsing, and teaching self-elevate themselves to a new and exciting creative level. You need to commit yourself to breath in the most unimaginable of ways, and you must believe in its power to both communicate and connect. Acceptance of audiation as a process in creating music is at the very foundation of all things musical. Audiation followed by breath moves musicing from the realm of imitating what was done before into the act of spontaneous creation and human expression.

Psychological acceptance of these principles is first and foremost. Allowing yourself to entrust to the breath "things" that you once believed were the purveyance of technique requires a major realignment of the musical thought process that you likely have spent a great deal of time acquiring. Of all the things I believe and know to be so, it is the miracle that is the breath informed by audiation that now precedes all I do musically. I allow my breath to do, and believe that my breath can do, all these things!

I love the phrase, "The easiest things are the hardest taught." In the world of music and conducting, there is nothing as simple in concept as the power of the breath, yet it is the hardest to comprehend or teach because it requires trust and belief, and therein lies the rub! To give into the power of one's audiation followed by breath is one of the rue miracles of our art.

Breath does carry all that we do, if we allow it to. It is in this allowing that we find ultimate challenge.

In the silence, I have everything or nothing, I am old, I am tired for seventy-five years. When you are not awake, I am weary, but when you are awakened, it is a privilege. It is so beautiful, this human mind. (p. 84)

The mind and the body should have been granted natural faculties. That goes without saying. But with the gifts alone, one cannot go very far. It is important to remember that the greater the gifts, the greater must be the character, the power of the work, the conscience, the moral and spiritual value of him to whom they were given. (p. 85)

—Nadia Boulanger
in *Master Teacher*

Each breath moment is its own universe. In meditation, we come to know something about this terrain in ways that open doors, that bring us back to our senses, that refine our hearts, that help us understand what it means to be human, what it means to be whole, right here, right now. (p. xi)

—Larry Rosenberg
in *Breath by Breath*

CHAPTER 10

BREATH AS INITIATOR

Music is not notes. Music is what the notes *do*. (p. 29)

—David McGill
in *Sound in Motion*

"Don't you cellists ever breathe? After all, the human voice learned to sing long before stringed instruments were invented. And singers must breathe. The audience also breathes. Play it again but this time humanize this long passage. Play it as though you, too, had to breathe while phrasing. Form it into bite-size phrases which the audience can assimilate comfortably while they, too, continue to breathe." (p. 133)

—George Szell, as quoted
by Philip Farkas
in David McGill,
Sound in Motion[5]

---

5   This incredible book by David McGill, bassoonist with the Chicago Symphony Orchestra, deciphers and analyzes the phrasing system as taught by the great oboist, Marcel Tabuteau, who taught at Curtis. Tabuteau's system is worth the time for thought and study because it gives clarity and humanity to the human idea contained in the breath.

The gait of man and beast, the flight of birds, the circulation
of the blood, and the breathing process are rhythmicized.
(p. 93)

> —Wilhelm Ehmann
> in *Choral Directing*

One thought only: rhythmic problems are not primarily
problems of reading—for us. We repeat things often enough
so that it should be difficult for a sightless person to make
more than a few mistakes. The primary problem is that of
feeling. Now, that is a fairly indeterminate "term," but what I'm
trying to say is that the "sense" of rhythm is a mighty complex
thing: physical, physiological, psychological, visceral,
etceteractual; and our problem as a group is not that of visual
identification—two quarter-notes equal one half-note—
but that of getting people to *experience* two quarter-notes
simultaneously physically, physiologically, psychologically,
viscerally and etceteractually. We turn the old grade school
apology, "I know what it is, but I can't put it into words," all
the way around. We can put rhythm into words—symbols—
but we have no idea what it is. (p. 65)

> —Robert Shaw
> in *The Robert Shaw
> Reader*

All life consists of rhythmic processes. From the simple pulsations of a single-cell organism to the rising and falling of our breath, life is filled with rhythm. This rhythm is also called "periodicity," meaning that the activity of something falls in cycles. Much of life is directed by the external rhythms of nature. For example, the earth spins on its axis and rotates around the sun, and around our moon orbits the earth. We attune ourselves to the cycles of the sun and the moon, following the different rhythms they create. With day and night, different behavior is created; we usually get up with daylight and go to sleep at night. When our light-dark cycle is disturbed, as when we take a long jet flight, our ability to function in the new environment is affected for a day or two. We call this "jet lag." Different behavior due to rhythm also occurs for the different seasons of the year and the response of nature to this. Not only our sleep patterns, but our eating patterns, digestive patterns, even our harvesting and mating patterns are affected by the rhythms of these cycles.

—Jonathan Goldman
from "Sonic Entrainment"
website: www.healingsounds com

The point being made throughout this book is that breath is a "carrier" of all things both human and musical. In considering the breath, one could certainly compartmentalize the discussions of the many influences breath has upon musicing. Among all of its influences, the ability of breath to set sound *in motion* is perhaps one of its most miraculous qualities. If you believe that music is sound in motion, then it behooves you to understand what initiates that motion.

ACTION-REACTION

When you breathe, the energy for what is to follow is initiated by the breath, and the breath alone. From a purely "architectural" point of view, the overall shaping and direction of any phrase is birthed in your breath. What follows in sound is merely and simply a reaction to the energy contained in the breath. The relationship of phrase to breath is a Newtonian physics "action-reaction" response. The breath is so powerful because it launches the phrase direction and phrase shape of what is to follow. In fact, all things dealing with the architecture of the phrase are launched within the breath inhalation and sustained through the subsequent exhalation.

One of the reasons breath has such a profound influence on what follows in musical performance has to do with another simple principle: the principle of entrainment. The breath assumes a powerful role in musicing because it sets up what is to follow musically in a very organic and powerful way. Breath not only has a wavelike effect upon the sounds that are birthed by the performer, but from the aspect of a conductor it also sets up a chain reaction of musical responses that shape the musical ideas that follow. To not acknowledge that the breath has such powers relegates music making to a process of manipulation and control as sound is being produced. That manipulative process creates, at worst, dishonest music and has immediate negative effects upon resonance, pitch and expressivity.

GAINING AN UNDERSTANDING OF
BREATH ENTRAINMENT

Think of entrainment as sympathetic resonance between bodies. Everything, including human beings, has resonances that can be set in motion when they either share similar frequencies or are allowed to accept the vibrating frequency of a larger group of objects or persons. In musicians, it is the breath that sets up the phenomenon of entrainment. In 1665, Dutch Physicist Christian Huygens discovered that if you have several clocks with pendulums of different lengths, after a period of time, no matter their size, all of the clocks would synchronize with each other.

Entrainment is also interactive. You can change the natural oscillatory patterns of one object (musician) and replace them with another (as initiated by breath). If you were aware of entrainment, you would see its effects everywhere. The connections could be anything, from a simple conversation between two people that is in the same "tempo" to a great public speaker and the response of a crowd being in the same tempo (i.e., Martin Luther King's "I Have a Dream" speech). All of those connections are established because of *breath*. In medicine there has been research concerning the effects of sound entrainment upon entrainment of both hemispheres of the brain. While the research has been somewhat limited, its conclusions point strongly to the profound and direct influence of entrainment upon our body rhythms and the energy that courses throughout us.

Sound entrainment has also been used in Tibetan meditation practice for centuries. Jeff Strong and The Rhythm Entrainment Institute maintains that rhythm patterns can be categorized for specific therapeutic results (calming, dyslexia, autism). His discussions and experimental data form a compelling case as to the power of entrainment. It is my contention that all of these "rhythm patterns" are established through the breath.

ENTRAINING MUSICAL IDEAS

If you consider that breath can set sound in motion, then it must follow that the sound set in motion can also at the same moment be charged with all of the other aspects of musical expression. Through score study and the study of vocal or instrumental technique, practice takes care of detail. In other words, taking care of detail through meticulous practice allows the details to eventually take care of themselves.

Technique and human ideas are magically bundled together at the moment of inhalation through a process of submitting oneself totally to the power of the breath. No logic, no thinking…just a simple "allowing" for the idea to be breathed is all that is required. The energy and spirit of the breath taken, laden with musical expression, immediately gives birth to sound that will have its own trajectory borne out of the human idea that was set in motion by both the idea and the energy of the breath. Decisions about the particulars of phrasing are determined and defined in the rehearsal and practice room. If such detail is dealt with through practice, then breath becomes the vehicle for musical expression. It is that simple, but unbelievably powerful, to allow the breath to do all of this. Breath binds all ideas about the architecture of musical phrases— the human idea and the composer's intent—and initiates those musical ideas in sound. Whether the singing of a children's choir, the playing of an elementary wind band, or the great singer of art song, it is breath that carries all to the listeners' ears and compels audiences to feel and believe in what is being performed.

> The theory handed down from the Pythagoreans seems to entail the same view; for some of them have declared that the soul is identical with the particles in the air, and others with what makes these particles move. These particles have found their place in theory because they can be seen perpetually in motion when the air is completely calm. Those who say that the soul is that which moves itself tend towards the same view. For they all seem to assume that movement is the distinctive characteristic of the soul, and that everything else owes its movement to the soul… (p. 21)

—Aristotle
in *On the Soul*

CHAPTER 11

WHERE IS "IN THE MOMENT"?

"Living in the moment" becomes, the more one thinks about it, a shabby phrase. But there is a very particular sense in which it represents wisdom. Not to be yourself, but to *see* yourself as you are in the present, unredeemed by acts past or future: that knowledge opens an avenue to moral clarity.

The stark judgment of the moment is a rigor meant for oneself alone, not for others. (p. 238)

—Richard Todd
in *The Thing Itself*

Musicians often talk of being "in the moment." They use the phrase like it is a religion, something to strive for and live by. Yet many never, if ever, define this semantic twist of the language. It sounds good. It seems right. But while this phrase may have a certain cache, I have always been bothered by how easily it could be misinterpreted and misused. Being "in the moment" could be a trap to lull you into believing that the moment is objective and quantifiable and exists unto itself. Unless narrowly defined, "in the moment" could lead you down a difficult musical path that makes your own personal and authentic musical voice difficult to access. At its worse, if you think that "in the moment" represents only the present moment, then it poses the danger of getting "stuck" in the moment!

PAST, PRESENT, AND FUTURE

To arrive at a more accurate picture of "in the moment," you must consider the perceptual dilemma of being a musician. At the moment of creation of a musical sound or phrase, there is the past, the present, and the future of any sound happening at the same time. This principle has been proven in the studies of the psychology of music. We are capable of hearing in three different dimensions simultaneously. The mistake many performing artists make is that they get "stuck" in the present moment. The musical "idea" gets lost in this cognitive trap, and the potential for any honest expression is severely muted, even dampened. The miracles of what happens when you breathe in an idea cannot and should not be hampered by trying to understand, or even being aware of, being "in the moment." By being "in the moment" as an aware cognitive point in time, you are exercising a strong sense of control over the innate spontaneousness of any artistic expression. You will also find yourself stuck in what rapidly becomes the past.

Consider this analogy with language. If you wanted to be "in the moment" when you speak, you would speak and be aware of every single word you are speaking as it is being spoken. In reality, there is no "in the moment" when you speak. If you were worried about being "in the moment," your speech would be reduced to hopeless, unintelligible stuttering. You cannot control human expression, but you can allow expression to grow out of the breath!

The quote that begins this chapter perhaps summarizes this dilemma the best. Those who are "in the moment" transform a communicative, artistic moment into a self-centered act by thinking and getting stuck in the moment. The breath and the power of the breath is the only thing that can liberate a performing artist into a state of honest artistic expression.

MIMETIC ENVY THAT HANDICAPS THE BREATH

There is a fine line between breathing an idea that is honest and breathing an idea that is taken in envy of a sound desired. Plato explored this dichotomy in great detail. Basically, it is close to "being in the moment." For Plato, if art is merely an imitation of life (or the "reenactment" of a previous performance), then musical expression become as re-presentation of something that is copied, not created! For Plato, this "re-presentation" is always removed from reality.[6] "In the

6   Sreenath Nair, *Restoration of Breath*, p. 11.

moment" thinking encourages re-presentation that has tinges of artistic dishonesty. The real artistic voice that is within is then stifled. Envy of sound via a duplication of what was previously performed robs the breath of its power to communicate.

CHAPTER 12

TOWARD A DEEPER ARTISTRY: BREATH IS UNTO ITSELF

Technique, wonderful sound...all of this is sometimes astonishing—but it is not enough. (p. 1)

> —Pablo Casals
> in David Blum,
> *Casals and the Art of*
> *Interpretation*

To the rationally minded, the mental process of the intuitive appears to work backward. His conclusions are reached before his premises. This is not because the steps which connect the two have been omitted but because those steps are taken by the unconscious. (p. 36)

> —Frances Wickes
> in Stephen
> Nachmanovitch,
> *Free Play*

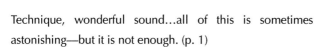

"As Western students of Oriental culture have discovered, the First Principle does not lend itself to precise translation," said my Chinese friend, an art historian. "It is something definite, yet it is indescribable. It is how you feel when you enter a room and sense that everything in it is somehow harmonious; you know that you are at peace there. It is how your life suddenly seems to change when you fall in love. It is the way in which your spirit comes into subtle accord with the movement of life around you; at the same time it is an experience within yourself—at the very centre. It is active and passive, embracing and releasing; it is a profound sense of being."

We were discussing *ch'i-yun*, the first of the Six Principles set down by the art critic Hseih Ho in the fifth century A.D. in what is thought to be the earliest document stating the fundamental canons of Chinese painting. It was maintained that in order to become a master, the artist must prove himself in the following skills: vitality of brushstroke, accuracy in portrayal, versatility in coloring, care in arrangement of composition, transmission of tradition through copying the works of earlier masters. But the foremost task lay in the fulfillment in the First Principle, which has sometimes been defined as "breath-resonance life-motion." For only by coming into harmony with the vital cosmic spirit or breath could the painter convey through the movement of his brush the mysterious vitality of life itself. (p. 1)

"The other five principles may be acquired through study and perseverance," said my friend, "but *ch'i-yun* comes from within. It develops in the silence of the soul." (p. 2)

—David Blum
in *Casals and the Art
of Interpretation*

The creation of something new is not accomplished by the intellect but by the play instinct acting from inner necessity. The creative mind plays with the objects it loves. (p. 42)

—Carl Jung
in Stephen Nachmanovitch,
Free Play

Inspiration may be a form of superconsciousness, or perhaps of subconsciousness—I wouldn't know; but I am sure that it is the antithesis of self-consciousness. (pp. 42–43)

—Aaron Copland
in *Music and Imagination*

Throughout my teaching career, I have encountered many situations that have given me pause to try to understand how to teach what we call "artistry." I have given a great deal of thought to how or what could grow such a way of being and creating within us. While there are no magic potions, deeper artistry (or any artistry, for that matter) lies in the breath. But the breath can only carry what we will it to carry in our musicing. And without the breath, musicing will only be a technical representation, a vague outline of the expression of a musical idea that demands more of us as teachers, conductors, and performing artists.

There is a great deal of belief, and some artistic security, that if we tend to our technical house, then our communicative expression will somehow magically appear in the sounds we make. As a musician, you must realize that those details are ever only the framework. Human expression is and can only be birthed in the breath. Musical intention, musical will, musical idea, and the connection with others (both other performers and those who hear the music) can only happen in the moments you breathe. What comes after the breath is mere execution. My colleague Nova Thomas speaks later in this book about re-languaging the breath. To build upon her idea, re-languaging the breath also means you must re-language your music creation process. You must believe that all of your human expressive capacity occurs in the moment of the breath and can only be carried by the breath.

Many musicians (including myself) become musically incapacitated at times because we just do not give breath and its power its musical due. We cannot for some reason give breath its rightful placeholder in our musical process. In addition, as a profession, we have not separated out breath as the specific element that is the sole carrier of our musical intent, our musical idea, and our very spirit.

It is fine to understand rehearsal process and to become a craftsman in the rehearsal room. We have all been told that technique is a "means to an end." But there has always been a mystery about that "end"— we most likely believed that the "end" in that process would just happen as long as we focused on our teaching and rehearsal technique. If we apply such logic to speaking, then as we speak (and even before we speak) we grammatically plot each sentence over and over again in our mind (i.e., our creative spoken ideas come out of graphing sentences). But we all know that's not the way it works. Spoken words, spoken ideas are all birthed in the moment when we breathe. As Thomas Hampson so eloquently stated, "We realize the idea of what we want to express and then breathe into that."

It is time to separate breath from technique in our mind. Consider the miracle of that silent stillness where idea becomes wedded to sound. Spend time developing that part of your "technique." Your interpretation of the music does not happen as you produce sound; it happens in the moment of breath. If you analyze what you do as a musician, it won't take much to realize that with every phrase, idea is carried by breath, and the execution of the sound is the bastion of technique. Technique is technique, but human expression is ignited in the breath. When you come to understand that breath and what it carries is truly unto itself and where human expression lies, then your artistry will soar and your ability to connect with others will create and honest and meaningful communication—the kind of communication that makes life worth living, and through which you can find a deeper understanding of what it means to be human.

PART II

INTERPRETATIONS AND APPLICATIONS

CHAPTER 13

THE CONDUCTOR'S INTIMATE CONNECTION TO BREATH

The third element of the triad, which St. Gregory called "blessedness," is unmistakable when it is present in the choir, when the perfect balance is found between silence and speech, action and contemplation, giving and receiving. This third element cannot be controlled. Its appearance is a gift, but a gift for which we must prepare. (p. 14)

—Rembert Herbert
in *Entrances: Gregorian Chant in Daily Life*

Considering the value of the argument that Aristotle establishes in terms of breath and its psycho-physical movements, it is obvious that each physical movement and each mental reflection must have a corresponding movement of breath in the body, linking physical activities and mental experiences together. (p. 57)

—Sreenath Nair
in *Restoration of the Breath*

For the qualities that distinguish *great* conductors lie far beyond and above what we have spoken of. We now begin to deal with the intangibles, the deep magical aspect of conducting. It is the mystery of relationships—conductor and orchestra bound together by the tiny but powerful split second. How can I describe to you the magic of the moment of beginning a piece of music? There is only one possible fraction of a second that feels exactly right for starting. (p. 160)

—Leonard Bernstein
in *The Joy of Music*

Conductors often talk about "connection" in their rehearsals and performances. That connection can happen at many different levels—for example, the spiritual connection between conductor and ensemble, which has and will continue to be the subject of much discussion and thought. But another, lesser-known connection is through an awareness of just how the conductor's gesture connects to the ensemble's breath.

This connection happens through four specific pathways:

1. Acceleration/deceleration of conducting gesture
2. The breath impulse gesture
3. Empathetic constant exhalation
4. The troughed beat

1. ACCELERATION/DECELERATION:
A MIRROR OF BREATH ENERGY AND FLOW

Perception of motion is a complicated psychological principle. There is a distinction between how a conductor perceives his or her own gestures and how the ensemble perceives the conductor's gestures. An ensemble lives in a world of reaction, and a conductor lives in a world of perceived movement, which is at best a sequence of smaller movements bundled together to convey direction to the ensemble.

As a conductor, you must analyze and understand the components that make up your conducting gesture, as well as your own perception of how you move with music and the impact those movements have on your ensemble. Conductors generally are not "movers" by nature, so they tend not to accurately perceive what they are doing at all times. By studying the concepts of acceleration and deceleration, you can clear the "perceptive smoke" from your kinesthetic sense.

The reality of gesture is that any conducting pattern is a subtle but specifically choreographed dance between accelerated and decelerated elements. Both acceleration and deceleration are present in every conducting pattern, and the constant interplay between acceleration and deceleration is what propels musical line. Acceleration affects tempo and the overall vocal health of the singers, and too much deceleration affects tempo, as well as pitch and vowel color. The interplay of acceleration and deceleration (i.e., the speed of the conducting gesture) directly affects the use of the air by both singers and instrumentalists!

2. THE BREATH IMPULSE GESTURE

A subtle deceleration in all gestures provides an empathetic movement that mirrors how the breath moves to the ensemble. Think of the traditional preparation gesture as a *breath impulse gesture*. Each breath impulse gesture involves two components: (1) the descent to the ictus (or chi), which accelerates to the chi, followed by (2) the upward movement at the moment of the ictus, which mirrors the breath falling into the body.

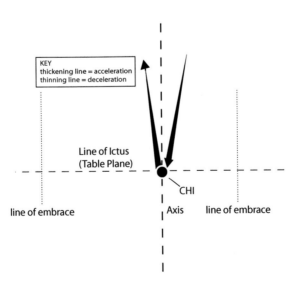

Breath enters the body at the moment of "chi," at the bottom of the preparatory breath impulse gesture as the arm and hand descend doward to "chi."[7] This breath impulse gesture occurs before the first beat of a piece; it takes the place of the generally accepted upward-moving preparatory gesture. The correct *feeling* during the second half of the dropped "V" impulse is that of deceleration. While subtle, the deceleration occurs because the conducting gesture is moving against gravity. Speed of deceleration directly influences the speed of the air being released by instrumentalists or singers. With instruments, the speed of air is determined by the playing technique of the instruments; with vocalists, the speed of air is more sensitive and affects vocal production of sound.

The breath impulse gesture is the physical manifestation of the moment when you begin to breathe in the *idea* that is bound to the breath. Remember that the opening of the body and the following breath initiate movement, a kind of pulsation that initiates many "things" within us. Consider the following:

> Aristotle describes the origin of breath as having its source within, either as a "function of the soul" or "soul itself or else some mixture of bodies which by their means cause this attraction" (*On Breath,* IV: 497). While thus linking breath and pulsation, Aristotle further asserts that breathing is a pulsation which is the primary act and "the underlying essence of animals." This means that, for Aristotle, pulsation, breath and soul are the fundamental principles interlinking the physical and the psychological experience of the body because movement and sensation are the two matching qualities through which the soul operates in the body (*On the Soul,* I. II: 29) (p. 56)

> —Sreenath Nair
> in *Restoration of the Breath*

---

7   The breath impulse gesture is demonstrated on the companion DVD to this text.

The role of the breath actually being the binding stuff of soul is clearly at the forefront of Aristotle's thoughts about breath:

> Those who have interpreted the soul in terms of motion have regarded the soul as most capable of producing movement. But those who have referred it to cognition and perception regard the soul as the first beginning of all things. (*On the Soul,* I. II: 23)
>
> ...For Aristotle, the soul on the one hand represents the idea of human embodiment, which is the physical basis of all the human experiences of mind and body. On the other hand, the soul is explained as the appearance of breath in the body which causes the functioning of movement, sensation and mind. (p. 56)

—Sreenath Nair
in *Restoration of the Breath*

3. EMPATHETIC CONSTANT EXHALATION

This technique has a profound effect upon the use of breath by performers. When musicians are producing sound, whether instrumentalists or singers, they are using air to produce that sound. Without realizing it, conductors directly impact how freely the performers use their air by how they themselves either hold or lock the air within their bodies as they conduct, or release their air into the sound of the ensemble. Holding the breath after inhalation of the idea mutes or destroys communication between conductors and ensembles.

If you hold your mouth closed and don't release air either through your nose or your mouth (or both), you create a negative effect upon the quality and freedom of the sound your ensemble produces. Musicians cannot counteract the effects of a non-exhalating conductor. If you do not exhalate as you conduct, you immediately affect how your ensemble is producing sound and how it is being released from their bodies or their instruments. Furthermore, the ensemble's almost intuitive reaction to your non-exhalation causes technical problems, such as intonation problems and problems pertaining to the free and healthy resonance in singers or the timbres of instrumentalists.

When conducting, always lightly exhale as if fogging a window. Inhale for Replenishment whenever necessary! These replenishing breaths are different from the breaths a conductor takes when breathing in empathy with singers or instrumentalists: replenishing breaths do not carry the idea; they simply replenish. So the conductor's breath is of two types: (1) empathetic (that breath taken at the same moment the musicians breathe and (2) replenishing (when the conductor replenishes his or her own breath for constant exhalation).

The effects of constant exhalation on the musicing process are profound and far-reaching. First, exhaling air provides a physiological logic for the conducting act. If you agree that conducting involves movement, then it follows that oxygen must be supplied to the muscles for free and unencumbered movement to occur. By not exhalating, you decrease the amount of oxygen going to your muscles, which causes rigidity in your muscles and your conducting movements.

There is a second, and perhaps even more powerful, effect upon musicians when the conductor employs this mode of constant exhalation. The effect is both physiological and spiritual. When you exhale, you are performing a powerful empathetic act upon the musicians in front of you. When you exhale, your ensemble immediately senses that they can more freely release their sound. If you do not exhale, you cause a powerful withholding of breath in your musicians. It is this withholding of breath that creates "held" sounds, which manifest themselves aurally as tight, resonantly dull, or out-of-tune sounds. To remedy this situation, you must check your exhalation process.

By exhalating when conducting, you are also able to provide, through your breath, a want to *give of yourself* "into" the sound of your ensemble. Exhalation, and the physical opening that comes with exhalation, is a direct physical manifestation of openness and vulnerability that is immediately and intuitively apparent to the musicians who sit in front of you! In other words, constant exhalation provides the most intimate of human connection between conductors and performers; it becomes a very intimate *connective tissue*[8] that binds and strengthens the musical experience. By not exhaling (and breathing), you create serious technical and human problems within your ensemble: over time, the effects of non-empathetic breathing and exhaling upon your musicians causes long-term technical damage and makes communication and connection between you and your ensemble more difficult. By constantly exhaling, you establish an immediate and deeply human connection to your ensemble.

BREATHING THE SCORE:
MARKING THE SCORE FOR REHEARSAL AND PERFORMANCE

Acknowledging that breathing is important to a conductor's art will cause immediate and profound changes in how you and your ensemble both rehearse and perform. This awareness will not only improve the technical aspects of music performance but also provide an organic foundation to music making and the connective human tissue that brings honesty into rehearsals and performances.

---

8   Mark Moliterno explains his use of this term on the companion DVD to this text.

But awareness and acknowledgment are simply not enough. You must set out on a path to make the mechanics of breathing clear. I have long admired the teaching of Margaret Hillis with regard to score marking. Margaret Hillis believed in the power of score "colorization," placing colored pencil to paper. By coloring a score, you obtain information through a sort of visual osmosis that may be hidden in a normal visual examination of the score.

THE BREATH PREPARATION

For entrances to be made with both technical and musical sanity, they must always be prepared by the conductor in the breath that precedes the entrance. Conductors have traditionally been taught that cueing initiates attack. While this may be true, the nature of that attack—its color, dynamic, intensity, and human content—can only be "prepared" by the conductor's breath that precedes it. The breath before any musical sound is the place to breathe the musical "idea" or "intention" into your open body. The size and spaciousness of that opening directly relates to the "soul" content of that space you are breathing into. If used to its fullest, the breath is able to carry and consequently influence the following musical/technical qualities of sound:

- Color of the sound
- Dynamic
- Tempo
- Consistency of tempo
- Rhythmic character
- Idea
- Phrase trajectory and phrase shape

It is not enough to merely believe you will remember when to breathe. You must comprehend as a conductor what it is to breathe for all persons in the ensemble. While you cannot truly breathe for all of them, it is reasonable to take on the responsibility of breath cueing as many entrances as possible. But tracking *every* breath preparation is very difficult without some level of score marking. It is hard to master this technique without marking the score in a unique and colored manner.

I advocate a very simple score marking technique. Using a highlighter (usually green), I draw a large vertical line through the rest or beat prior to the entrance. I train myself that this breath preparation is a physical two-step process: I *open* my body prior to the highlighted beat and breathe into my musical idea prior to each parts entrance, and I continue to exhale until the next breath preparation. In most instances, I also mark the start of my inhalation process with a light ictus in my hand at the moment of inhalation.[9]

Two examples of breath marking a score are shown on the pages that follow. Whether instrumental or choral, you should mark the individual breaths of your instrumentalists or singers in your score. Since the body of this book is printed in black and white, the shaded vertical lines represent the lines that would appear in a highlighted color. The examples are two versions of the same familiar work: the first is the marked choral score of Morten Lauridsen's *O Magnum Mysterium* (Peer), and the second is an excerpt from the transcription of that work by H. Robert Reynolds (Peer).

---

9   This breath impulse technique is demonstrated on the companion DVD to this text.

THE FOLLOWING EXCERPT IS FROM THE CHORAL OCTAVO

O MAGNUM MYSTERIUM
BY MORTEN LAURIDSEN

PEER MUSIC: 61860-121
USED BY PERMISSION OF SONGS OF PEER, LTD.

NOTE:
SHADED AREAS MARKED IN THE FOLLOWING SCORE EXCERPT INDICATE POINTS OF INHALATION
FOLLOWED BY EXHALATION.

O Magnum Mysterium

Morten Lauridsen

2227209

2

4

THE FOLLOWING EXCERPT IS FROM THE FULL SCORE
FOR CONCERT BAND

O MAGNUM MYSTERIUM
BY MORTEN LAURIDSEN
TRANSCRIBED BY H. ROBERT REYNOLDS

PEER MUSIC
USED BY PERMISSION OF SONGS OF PEER, LTD.

NOTE:
SHADED AREAS MARKED IN THE FOLLOWING SCORE EXCERPT INDICATE POINTS OF INHALATION
FOLLOWED BY EXHALATION.

O Magnum Mysterium

Morten Lauridsen
transcribed for band by H. Robert Reynolds

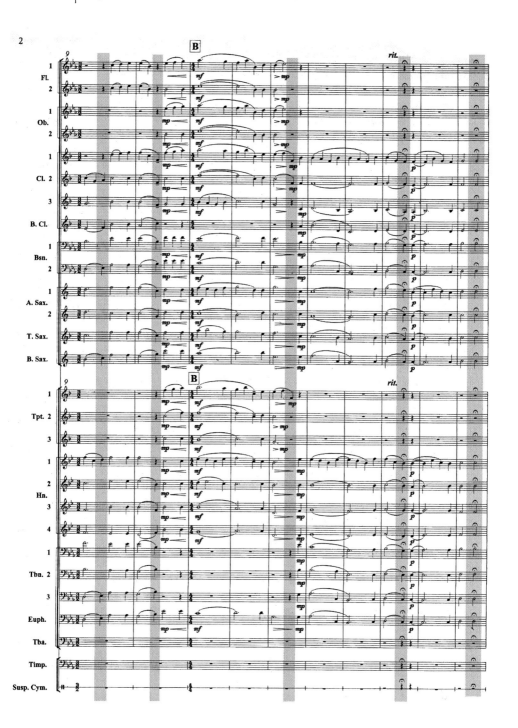

4. THE TROUGHED BEAT

I use the term "troughed beat" to describe to my conducting students the kinesthetic act of connecting physical conducting gesture to sound. But in re-examining my use of this term, it is perhaps more appropriate to talk about connecting gesture to *breath*.

Through the years there has been much attention on the downbeats and upbeats in conducting gesture. But the miracle of conducting is what happens in the moment of "chi," or the bottom of the beat as the beat changes direction, as shown in the illustration below.

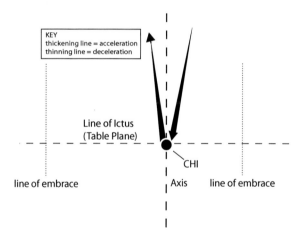

Tataki begins from a preparatory position as a preparatory motion, and travels upward with a smooth deceleration. At the instant the arm has decelerated to a complete stop, it begins to fall, accelerating smoothly, until it sharply strikes the predictable point (the bottom of the field of the beat). In other words, it imitates in the air the motion of a ball bouncing sharply on a floor. Further, the decelerating motion after the Point serves as a preparatory motion to the next beat. (p. 9)

—Hideo Saito
in *The Saito Conducting Method*

As Hideo Saito, the great conducting pedagogue has pointed out, an "ictus" or "chi" is a change of direction that coincides with a release of energy. The moment of "chi" provides the opportunity for conductors to physically connect with the breath of their musicians!

> After mastering the sharp-upward bursting motion, you must learn to relax the muscle immediately after the burst, while the arm continues to move upward. Use the energy of the initial burst to raise your arm smoothly with a natural deceleration to the level of your head. It is important that the motion appear natural. In other words, from the initial burst to the apex of the motion, where the arm has completely decelerated, the motion must be continuous, without jerkiness, and free from any unnatural movement. (p. 15)

> —Hideo Saito
> in *The Saito Conducting Method*

Consider the beat "points" or "points of arrival" within a beat pattern. For purposes of illustration, let's look at a four-beat legato pattern (shown below).

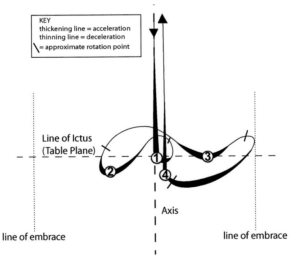

Most conductors are taught at these beat points to either "click" or simply change direction to demarcate tempo. Looking deeper, these are the points (or "chi") where you can connect directly with your ensemble's sound when conducting. The amount and degree of this connection depends on the quality of resonance and sostenuto desired in your ensemble. First, imagine a trough-like cup or indentation (as shown below) that you could place your hand into that is filled with a thick, gel-like substance.

Now place one of these "imaginary" troughs on each beat point of the legato pattern (as illustrated below).

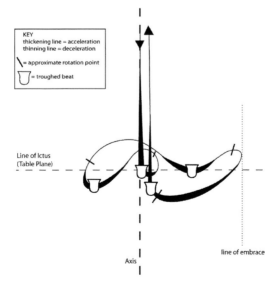

Conduct through the legato pattern, but imagine placing your hand in the gel-like substance contained in each trough. This is similar to a tenuto conducting gesture, but you add the dimension of connection (by placing your hand into the gel-like substance), which is representative of the breath stream of your ensemble. You may go as shallow or as deep into the trough as the musical line requires. But by going into the trough, you connect directly with the breath of the ensemble and reinforce singing and playing that is "on the breath" or "connected" to the breath stream. This physical kinesthetic connection, achieved through imagination, creates a connection to the ensemble sound that is unmistakable. Singers feel it, and instrumentalists certainly sense it. This can become one of the most valuable aspects of your personal conducting technique. This intimate connection between breath and hand is one of the miracles of what we do as conductors.

CHAPTER 14

Breath, the Mind/Body Connector:
A Classical Yoga Perspective
on the Creative Process

Mark Moliterno

Man and woman, beast and bird, live by breath.
Breath is therefore called the true sign of life.
It is the vital-force in everyone
That determines how long we are to live.

—Taittiriya Upanishad 3.1

Breath is energy.

Artistic expression in music is the result of a coordinated effort between a musician's internal creative intent, breath energy, and physical activity. These elements have a synergistic relationship to one another, and the breath has a vital role: it is the energetic circuit, the "connective tissue," between the artist's internal intention and external, physical expression. In other words, when a musical idea is conceived in the heart and mind of an artist, it is the breath that gives it life in the body, animating the physical instrument. If, in this process, the breath is not free to make the connection, the creative-physical gesture will be impeded. The breath is the energy, the vital-force, that unifies the mind and body in the musical act.

The concept of the breath as the mind-body connector may be somewhat unfamiliar within our culture, yet it is commonly understood in various Eastern philosophical traditions. In Classical Yoga,[10] for instance, breath is viewed as part of the energetic field that lies between the mind and body, and which communicates with both. This relationship is explained in the *Taittiriya-Upanishad* through the paradigm of the *koshas* (lit. "sheaths" or layers).

The *koshas* are understood to represent layers of human personality and individuality that surround a core of absolute consciousness, often referred to as the "true" or "universal" Self. In the broadest sense, according to Yoga philosophy, we each possess, and therefore share, the Self, and we also each possess the sheaths that cover the Self and give

---

10 Classical Yoga is one of the great philosophic traditions of India. It is a systematic program of ethical, physical, energetic, and meditative practices based upon ancient primary source materials (i.e., The Yoga Sutras of Patanjali, The Bhagavad Gita, The Upanishads) and intended to unify the various aspects of human nature within the practitioner. The term "yoga" literally means "union" or "yoking." Most fundamentally in Western culture, this is understood as the union of mind and body. For the musician, a Classical Yoga practice can develop the unitive connections between the mind, emotions, and physical self that ultimately lead to authentic musical expression.

us our individual natures. The layers, then, represent all aspects of our human condition: spiritual, intellectual, mental, energetic, and physical. The model of the *koshas* has value for us as musicians if we examine it to gain an understanding of how the mind-breath-body complex interacts when we are involved in the creative activity of music making.

According to the *kosha* paradigm, every human being begins with a spiritual consciousness, a true Self, which is then explained by the intellect, guided by the mind, energized by breath patterns, and expressed in the body. It is the goal of Yoga to balance and harmonize these various aspects of one's self to fully express the Self.

To visualize the *koshas,* think of them as a set of concentric circles emanating from the central core of spirit/consciousness/creativity in an outward expanse, culminating in the physical manifestation, the human body (as shown below).

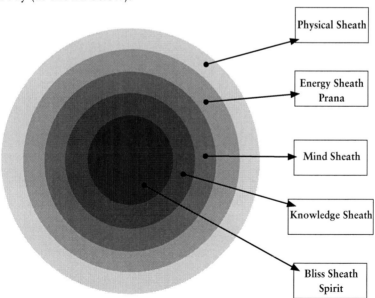

Each sheath covers, yet is supported by, the one below (interiorly) and conjoins with the one above (externally). Each layer is dependent upon the other layers for support and information, and there is a natural movement from the most subtle levels of the internal Self to the less subtle external level of the body.

At the center of the *kosha* diagram is the **Bliss Sheath**, representing the Self. It is the subtlest of the five *koshas* and, as such, is generally not accessed on a conscious level in everyday human experience. Yoga teaches that it is present in every person and is the foundation of who we are as a collective race; it represents the universal, creative principle, rooted in absolute peace and joy, which imbues all of humanity. In contemporary language, we may use the terms "spirit," "creative center," or "bliss state" to describe the Self, and depending upon the belief system, one may view this aspect of himself or herself in a spiritual way. As musicians, the Self is the "center" we are striving to identify, touch, and incorporate in authentic musical artistry, the essential creativity in each of us that we share when we make music together. In this view, music making is a spiritual activity that is manifested as physical expression.

From the level of absolute consciousness grows human intellect, discernment, and wisdom, represented by the **Knowledge Sheath**. This *kosha* is sometimes referred to as the "intuitive mind." It is in this realm that the performing artist makes interpretive decisions based on knowledge gleaned from study, as well as on the intuitive understanding of a composer's musical language.

Knowledge, in turn, supports the mind, represented by the **Mind Sheath**, which organizes the information received from the senses. Because it has such a close connection to the senses, this layer holds the relationship of the thoughts to the emotions; we respond and react to the information we receive from the outside world via our eyes, ears, etc. This is an important understanding for the musician because thoughts and emotions have a direct effect on a person's energy, and consequently on how a musical and/or dramatic idea is portrayed.

The **Energy Sheath** is an outgrowth of the mind and represents the presence of the universal life-force in every person. This energy is known in Yoga terminology as *prana*. It is the bio-energy found in all aspects of the natural world; *prana* propels a flower to grow from its seed toward the sun. In human beings, *prana* is the vital-force that is the essence of creativity. The Energy Sheath is the also the home of the breath.

Prana and breath animate the physical body; hence, the Energy Sheath connects to and supports the **Physical Sheath**. This is the most external, and therefore least subtle, *kosha*—the aspect of Self a person sees and identifies with on a daily basis. It is the realm in which the musician manifests such internal inspirational, intellectual, and emotional impulses as sound, communication, and art.

BREATH AND PRANA

The breath inhabits the Energy Sheath and is intimately integrated with *prana*. In fact, there is no authoritative reckoning within Yoga philosophy of a distinction between the two. *Prana* and breath are commonly understood to be so closely related that, for all intents and purposes, within the physical body, they are the same. Yet breath may be viewed as an agent for *prana* because breathing patterns affect *pranic* flow in the body. Breath is able to access, develop, move, and ultimately control one's life-force, and it does so either by one's conscious control (as in the practice of *pranayama[11]*) or as a less-conscious response to the impulses of the mind.

This relationship between mind, breath, and body is easy to understand if you consider the effects of your thoughts and emotions on your body in a stressful situation, for example, when you experience performance anxiety. In this condition, your state of mind (fear) blocks the natural flow of *prana* by stimulating the sympathetic nervous system.[12] When *prana* is blocked, breathing is also affected, becoming labored and unstable, and there is a resulting manifestation in the body: tension. The sensation of "butterflies in the stomach,"[13] or the inability to access a fluid breath, are the likely physical reflections of the performer's thoughts and emotions in that moment, and it is for this reason that the commonly prescribed antidote for performance anxiety is deep, steady breathing. Deep breathing stimulates the parasympathetic nervous system, reintegrates the flow of *prana*, calms the mind and emotions, and consequently reduces physical tension as well as mental disharmony. If you relate this mind-body phenomenon to the model of the *koshas*, you can understand that the innermost aspects of a person have a direct effect on his or her outermost aspects. The mind influences the breath which, in turn, effects how the body is energized.

---

11 *Pranayama* is the fourth limb of the eightfold path mentioned in the *Yoga Sutras of Patanjali*. One of the benefits of *pranayama* (lit. "life-force restraint") is the ability to control the mind as one learns to control his/her breathing.

12 The sympathetic nervous system supports the "fight or flight" reaction when we experience a sense of threat. The parasympathetic nervous system supports relaxation and balance within the internal organs for optimal health and a sense of well-being.

13 The solar plexus, located in the region of the heart, diaphragm, and stomach, is a large network of sympathetic nerves which, in part, govern the digestive system. Under emotional stress, such as performance anxiety, these nerves can manifest excitation as a feeling of agitation or tightness in the stomach and abdominal cavity.

People who regularly practice Yoga techniques such as *asana* (postures) and *pranayama* (breath control) develop an awareness of the subtle movements of their minds and how these movements relate to their breath and physical states. They begin to recognize that the breath connects the layers of mind and body, and energizes the deeper intentions of the spirit, intellect, and mind to become physical gesture. On the external level, Yoga practitioners gain conscious mastery over their physical bodies, recognizing tensions when they emerge, and they have specific strategies for releasing those tensions with the conscious use of their breath. They harmonize their minds and bodies with and through the breath.

Yoga teaches us how the breath makes this mind-body union possible and shows us the potential for its application in the lives and work of musicians. When a person experiences a sense of simultaneous harmony throughout the various aspects of himself or herself, we might say that person is embodying a conscious breath, an *authentic* breath. In fact, without this harmony in the entire system, the deeper aspects of a person will not be stable or accessible. For the artist, this means there will be limitations to the full range and depth of one's creativity. However, when a musician has trained himself or herself to embody an authentic breath and to use the power of that breath for connecting the various aspects of the Self, then the potential for creative expression is as limitless as the very life-force the breath is carrying.

BLOCKAGES TO THE BREATH

Authenticity in performing, then, is present when breath is free to energize the body to communicate the mental/emotional intention; the spirit, intellect, mind, breath, and body work together to manifest an artist's full creativity. When any aspect of the person sets conditions that block the breath from making the appropriate connections between the mental and physical *koshas*, the creative gesture is impeded. Blockages to the breath may correspond to imbalances in one or more of the *koshas*: physical (body tension), energetic (improper breath mechanics), mental (fear), intellectual (confusion), or spiritual/creative (conflicted beliefs). Yet, regardless of the cause, breath blockages are most commonly recognized at the level of the physical body by the presence of tension.

Generally speaking, physical blockages to the breath can be located in three areas of the torso:

1. The chest/shoulders/upper back
2. The ribs/solar plexus/thoracic spine
3. The abdominal wall/hips/pelvis and sacrum

Physical tension can be present in one or more of these areas when a musician performs. For this reason, the emphasis on technical mastery in the performing arts is understandable: a good technique should eliminate physical tensions. However, when tension *is* present, the breath is blocked from its ability to carry creative energy between the mind and body. Yoga practices balance and eventually eliminate the physical blocks to a free breath. When blocks are removed, the individual is able to access deeper states of consciousness and creativity through authentic breathing.

Exercise:
Evaluate your breathing patterns.

- Sit comfortably on the floor with your legs crossed, or on a chair with your feet on the floor. Make sure your back is straight and your head is balanced on top of your spine.
- Observe your normal breath pattern. Is it:
    Slow or fast?
    Deep or shallow?
    Smooth or jerky?
    Fluid or held?
- Once you become aware of your breathing, try to take a conscious, deep breath. Observe whether or not this is easy for you to do.
    - Do you feel an expansion of the torso on the inhalation, from the abdomen to the collarbones?
    - Does the breath catch at any point along the way?
- Now try to exhale evenly and slowly. Again, notice if there is a physical freedom to the breath, or if there are areas of tension that prohibit a fluid and complete exhalation.
- Observe your breathing in this way for five to ten full, deep breath cycles. Notice areas of tension or blockage and try to work through them on the next breath.

- Let your breathing return to normal. Notice any changes in your normal breath pattern from when you began the exercise.
- Become aware of tensions that are present in your breathing, both during a normal breath and in conscious, full breathing. Begin to become aware of possible causes for these tensions/blockages. Is there any information you can take from the model of the *koshas* to help explain the source of any blockage to your breath?

PRANAYAMA (BREATH/VITAL-FORCE CONTROL)

Prana is conveyed in the mind-body by and through a person's breathing patterns. *Pranayama,* then, is the practice of retaining, controlling, and distributing the vital-force through the use of specific breathing techniques. Conscious breathing in *pranayama* exercises regulates internal health, stimulates greater self-awareness, and consciously connects you to your body.

The Musician's Breath DVD (a partner to this book) provides an overview of three common *pranayama* practices: three-part breathing, active abdominal breathing (*kapalabhati*), and alternate nostril breathing (*nadi-shodhana*). In addition to the explanations given on the DVD, precise instructions for each of these practices are also offered below. For optimal understanding of the practices, use these directions in conjunction with the teaching on the DVD, paying specific attention to the **Practice Intention** for each exercise.

Pranayama practices usually take a while to master, but you might make observations about the mind-breath-body connection almost immediately. Start slowly and, over time, work your way up to an increased number of repetitions in each of the exercises. The best way to discover what the practices hold for you is to try them with a clear and pure intention.

Here are some basic principles for practicing *pranayama*:

- Warm the body first with Yoga postures or with physical movement.
- Practice breathing techniques before breakfast or two hours after eating.
- Wear comfortable, loose clothing and practice in a well-ventilated room.
- Make sure your counts are steady and unforced; use a metronome if you would like to have an external aid to counting.
- Concentrate your attention solely on your breathing. If other thoughts begin to creep in, gently bring your awareness back to the breath.
- If you have any questions or concerns about beginning a breathing practice, consult a doctor.

THREE-PART BREATHING

Three-part breathing is a foundational *pranayama* exercise. Consistent practice builds awareness of the breath cycle (inhalation, exhalation, retention), develops full capacity of the lungs, trains the mind to focus on a single objective, and improves overall health.

- Sit comfortably in a cross-legged posture or recline on the floor.
- Become aware of your normal, habitual breathing pattern and also the nature of your thoughts.
- Begin to breathe evenly, in three parts, inhaling first into the abdomen, then the ribs, and finally filling the chest (inhaling from bottom of the torso to the top). Inflate your lungs fully.
- Exhale contracting the abdomen, ribs, and then the chest (exhaling from bottom to top). Exhale fully.
- Become aware of blockages (tension) in any of the three areas of the torso. Repeat the breath cycle as fluidly as possible.
- Keeping an internal count or pulse, concentrate on the conscious, steady distribution of the breath into the abdomen, ribs, and chest in three equal parts (e.g., four counts in each of the three areas). If you notice blockages, try to consciously steady the breath to work through and past them.
- When you are comfortable and the breath is steady, evenly increase your counts in each of the three areas (e.g., increase from four to five counts).

- Become aware of the moment of transition between the inhalation and exhalation phases of the breath cycle. If you are comfortable, try to retain the breath after the inhalation phase and enjoy the absorption of *prana* in your body before beginning the exhalation. Retain the breath only to the point that you can still begin the exhalation comfortably. If you gasp to exhale, you've gone too far in the retention phase.

- Practice up to ten breath cycles for one set. Let the breath return to normal.

- Become aware of the nature and quality of your thoughts, the movement of mind and breath. Is there a relationship between how you feel and how your breath is moving?

- Work your way up to three sets of ten breaths.

Practice Intention:

Discover your natural breathing rhythm and then begin to gain conscious control of your breath energy. Become aware of the breath as the bridge between your mind and body. As you develop the ability to retain the breath after inhalation, try to allow the mind to rest in that moment, without movement. Begin to develop a sense of this moment as a transition between the expansion of your consciousness (inhalation) and the return to the point of its origin (exhalation). Receive an increased sense of peacefulness and well-being from this practice.

ALTERNATE NOSTRIL BREATHING (CHANNEL-BALANCING)

Alternate nostril breathing balances the energy channels that run along the right and left sides of the spine (*nadis*),[14] develops conscious control of the breath cycle, and balances the nervous system.

Most people find that one nostril is more open than the other and that it may even be difficult to breath through one side. This is normal. The two channels continually switch their dominance throughout the course of normal, daily activity. If you consider that each channel is energy-based, this may explain fluctuations in your energy at various points in your day.

- Sit comfortably in a cross-legged posture with your back straight and your head relaxed on top of your spine. (You can sit with your back against a wall for support and comfort.)
- Place your right index and middle fingers in your right palm with the thumb, ring, and pinky fingers extended.
- Inhale deeply through both nostrils. Then, closing your right nostril with your right thumb, slowly exhale through the left nostril.
- Keeping the right nostril closed, inhale slowly through the left.
- Close the left nostril with the ring and pinky fingers, open the right nostril, and slowly exhale.
- After full exhalation, slowly inhale again through the right side.

---

14 The *nadis* are channels for the flow of *prana*. *Ida nadi* begins in the base of the spine and winds its way up the spine to exit the left nostril. *Ida* represents feminine energy, a cooling quality, and may be related to the moon. *Pingala nadi* also begins in the base of the spine and ascends similarly to the right nostril. *Pingala* represents masculine energy, a warming quality, and may be related to the sun.

- Close the right side with the thumb, open the left side, and exhale slowly.
- Repeat for several rounds (up to ten), concentrating on maintaining an even count of both inhalation and exhalation as you alternate the nostrils.
- After your final breath cycle, remove your hand and take several deep breaths through both nostrils. Observe a feeling of balance in your breathing.

Practice Intention:

Become aware of how the mind controls the movement of your breath by developing concentration over the airflow between the right and left nostrils. If you experience any blockages to the fluid, steady and slow movement of the inhalation and exhalation, consciously try to smooth out any "bumps" along the way. Try to be sensitive to the balance of energy and the flow of prana between your right and left breath/ energy channels. Receive internal balance from this practice.

ACTIVE ABDOMINAL BREATHING (*KAPALABHATI*)

The name of this exercise, *kapalabhati*, is variously translated as "fire-breathing" and/or "skull shining breath" because it generates heat in the body and can cause a sensation of brightness in the mind or light-headedness. For this reason, you should always practice active abdominal breathing while seated (but never while driving!). This technique develops and tones the abdominal muscles, warms the body, purifies the blood stream, clears the nasal passages, and trains the mind to focus on the impulse of exhalation.

- Sit comfortably in a cross-legged posture with your back straight and your head relaxed on top of your spine. (You can sit with your back against a wall for support and comfort.)
- Place your hands on your knees or on your lower abdomen.
- Draw your navel strongly and quickly toward your spine, exhaling forcefully through the nose. Try to eliminate all tension from the chest and throat as you forcefully exhale: the impulse for the exhalation comes from the lower abdominal wall alone.
- Let your abdomen release passively for a light inhalation.
- Repeat 10 to 21 times for one round.
- When you are done with one round, take three deep, even breaths.
- Repeat the exercise twice more with three deep breaths between each set.

- Allow your breath to return to normal. Observe any
  sensations in your body and any change in the quality of
  your thoughts. If you are at all light-headed, take time to
  fully recover before starting any other activity.

Practice Intention:

Observe the impulse for exhalation as it begins in the
lower abdominal region. Develop a simultaneous ability
to energize the abdominal muscles while remaining free
and non-restricted in the throat, shoulders, and chest
as you exhale. Become sensitive to the clarity of mind
that follows the exercise. Receive physical vitality and
mental acuity from this practice.

BREATH AND BODY MOVEMENT

In relating breathing to body movement, one can make some
important observations. As a general rule, an inhalation opens the
body and creates a sense of expansion, while an exhalation tends to
promote a sense of contraction or release in the body.[15] Put another
way, you might say that the inhalation opens your consciousness in an
outwardly expansive gesture, while the exhalation returns you to your
center. Yoga uses the practice of physical postures (*asana*) to develop
the body for authentic breathing and to connect the movements of one's
consciousness with the gestures of one's body.

---

15 Think of a deep sigh when you are tired or stressed. A deep inhalation opens you to allow air to enter
the body, while the exhalation releases the fatigue or tension, sending it out of the body on the breath.

The human spine is essentially capable of movement in five directions: upward, backward, forward, side-to-side, and twisting. Understanding how the inhalation and exhalation phases of the breath cycle affect spinal movement is an important benefit of *asana* practice; one learns how the breath energizes physical movement. The following guidelines are reliable for coordinating your breath with spinal movement in Yoga postures:

- **Inhalation** promotes both **upward** and **backward-bending** spinal movement.
- **Exhalation** promotes both **forward-bending** and **twisting** spinal movement.
- Both **inhalation** and **exhalation** are equally important during **side-bending** spinal movement.

In addition, the movements of the spine have corresponding relationships to the three areas of potential breath blockage discussed above (chest, ribs, and abdomen):

- **Upward** movement of the spine affects **all three areas.**
- **Backward** bending affects the **chest and ribs.**
- **Forward** bending affects the **abdomen and ribs.**
- **Spinal twists** affect all three areas, especially the **ribs and thoracic spine.**
- **Side-to-side** bending affects the **ribs and chest.**

Yoga postures can be understood in the context of how each posture affects spinal movement, how the breath is coordinated with that particular movement, and what the positive effects of the movement are on the breath mechanism itself.

The *asana* practice on *The Musician's Breath* DVD is intended to be a starting point for your own personal exploration of your breath and its coordinated movement with your spine and body. For the Yoga postures portion of the program, I instruct a group of participants, most of whom had never tried Yoga before, in practices designed to address the issues outlined in this chapter. You are encouraged to begin with this program, evaluate the effects of the practices on your own mind-breath-body complex, and use it as a catalyst for further study and personal exploration.

Here are some guidelines for practicing Yoga postures:

- Wear loose, comfortable clothing.
- Practice in a well-ventilated, clean environment.
- Use a Yoga mat. Towels may slip and cause instability in certain postures.
- Practice Yoga postures before breakfast or two hours after eating.

Practice the Yoga *asanas* with the intention of understanding the role of the breath as the mind-body connector in each posture. Concentrate on the experience of the breath throughout your body, and evaluate the breath based on the following criteria:

Is the breath...

- smooth or jerky?
- slow or fast?
- deep or shallow?
- fluid or held?

By developing a conscious sensitivity to the location, direction, and flow of the breath in the Yoga postures, you will begin to identify any physical blockages that may be preventing a smooth, slow, deep, and fluid breath.

Notice how the breath affects your energy in various Yoga postures. On a still more subtle level, notice any corresponding thoughts, emotions, or attitudes that may emerge as you practice. What is the relationship of your body posture and breath to your thoughts and feelings?

Like any new technique, developing breath awareness in Yoga exercises requires practice. Be patient with yourself as you explore the practices; even experienced Yoga practitioners know there is always something new to learn. Try to approach the practices with an open, non-competitive mind that is ready to receive what the exercises have to teach you. Remember, too, that one of the foundational principles of Yoga is the ethical belief in *non-injury*: be kind to yourself as you explore and learn about your breath.

Namaste.[16]

---

16 Literally: "The light in me honors the light in you." This is a traditional, everyday greeting in India.

BIBLIOGRAPHY

Aranya, Swami Hariharananda. *Yoga Philosophy of Patanjali.* Trans.
    P.N. Mukerji. Albany: State University of New York Press,
    1983.

Butera, Robert. *The Pure Heart of Yoga: Ten Essential Steps for
    Personal Transformation.* Woodbury, MN: Llewellyn, 2009.

Coulter, H. David. *Anatomy of Hatha Yoga: A Manual for Students,
    Teachers, and Practitioners.* Honesdale, PA: Body and Breath,
    2001.

Feuerstein, Georg. *The Shambhala Encyclopedia of Yoga.* Boston:
    Shambhala, 1997.

Govindan, Marshall. *Kriya Yoga Sutras of Patanjali and the Siddhas.*
    Eastman, Quebec, Canada: Kriya Yoga Publications, 2000.

Hatha Yoga Pradipika: Light on Hatha Yoga. Trans. Swami
    Muktibodhananda. Mungar, Bihar, India: Yoga Publications
    Trust, 1998.

Swami Rama, Rudolph Ballentine, Alan Hymes. *Science of Breath.*
    Honesdale, PA: Himalayan Institute Press, 1998.

The Upanishads. Trans. Eknath Easwaran. Canada: Nilgiri, 2008.

CHAPTER 15

The Performer's Breath

Nova Thomas

The flow of breath is the flow of *presence* and *absence* and therefore, the flow of breath is the flow of meaning. Breathing is a movement that connects physical and mental activities together and therefore, it is a movement of action, meaning, and experience. The flow of breath is the passage of *time* that brings words, movements of the body, human actions, and thoughts into contact with each other in its place...Breath is *bio-theatricality* and the *invisible Other* that reinforce meaning into performativity. (pp. 46–47)

—Sreenath Nair
in *Restoration of Breath*

> Singing is so intimately bound up with the physical process of
> respiration, it is little wonder that the art of phonation touches
> upon the very essence of life itself. (p. 106)
>
> —Cornelius L. Reid
> in *Voice: Psyche and Soma*

There are as many pedagogical procedures and systems of management for the functional mechanics of breathing and "breath management" as there are pedagogues and singers. Back breathing, belly breathing, costal breathing, thoracic breathing, clavicular breathing, nose breathing, sustained breathing, appoggio, tucking, leaning, sipping, sighing, flowing, withholding, locking, unlocking—the verbiages, as well as the techniques and belief systems that support them, seem endless. In a discussion on breath and breath management in *The Naked Voice*, author W. Stephen Smith states that "the various approaches range from 'Don't think about breathing at all' to the most complicated and intricate understanding of the musculature involved and how to manipulate the muscles for proper breath support." Smith further postulates that although none of these techniques are necessarily wrong, they are "simply descriptions of what *happens* when we sing correctly, not what we *do* to sing right."[17] Theorist and teacher Cornelius L. Reid, in his exhaustive dictionary of vocal terminology, details what he believes to be fallacies in breathing techniques designed to "support" the tone.

---

17 W. Stephen Smith, *The Naked Voice* (Oxford University Press, 2007), p. 34.

The utilitarian value of breath support as a pedagogic practice is highly suspect. It is not based upon a valid functional principle, it leads to a self-conscious awareness of the body, confuses ends with means, and overlooks the fact that in an ideal technique all of the muscular systems involved are in equilibrium, which means that they are self-supporting. (p. 43)

—Cornelius L. Reid
in *A Dictionary of Vocal Terminology*

Smith and Reid are not alone in their ideas, but for these two fine pedagogues, there are scores of other fine pedagogues and singers who claim breath management to be the first and foremost consideration of singing technique. All vocal pedagogy books and treatises on singing have at least one chapter devoted to the subject, and every singer in the world deals with it, in one way or another. The various functional tenets of breath management and breathing technique (whether to have, or have not) have been thoroughly vetted across several populations. There is little, if anything, that this co-author can contribute to a discussion on mechanics and management. My own usage as a singer is based upon a system of "appoggio" that varies according to the vocal, musical, and dramatic circumstances of the moment; and my practice as a teacher of singers and actors is founded in the commitment to "remain curious" as to what particular way of thinking and behaving best serves the individual student. The proverbial roads to Rome are many.

The spirit of this book and its extraordinary author, James Jordan, invite different (I would argue, *deeper*) ways of looking at *breath* (as opposed to *breathing*)—ways that are certainly more inclusive and holistic. Breath is braided with meaning and expression, and there is at the core of Dr. Jordan's intentions a commitment to empower the expresser. Techniques for the mechanics of function give way, and sway, to more *artistic* considerations.

THE PSYCHO-PHYSICAL CONNECTION

My work as a singer and teacher of singers has been greatly advanced by my work as a teacher of actors. The Actors Studio Drama School, the New School for Drama, and Westminster College of the Arts have offered me living laboratories, in the form of classrooms, for the discovery of substantive ways to marry mechanics to meaning. Dramatic considerations for the actors of both spoken and lyric theaters have necessitated, and thankfully fostered, ways to synthesize technical and functional needs with opportunities for expression.

Konstantin Stanislavsky (1863–1938), the father of contemporary acting, marshals the inextricable connection between mind and body. He echoes Théodule Ribot's (1839–1916) assertion that a disembodied emotion is a non-existent one. Stanislavsky insists that in every physical action there is something psychological, and in the psychological, something physical. He goes even further to assert that there is an organic connection between body and soul. This connection is so strong, he insists, that…respiration revives not only flesh, but the life of the human spirit.[18]

Michael Chekhov (1891–1955), referred to by Stanislavsky as "his most brilliant student," and widely regarded to be one of the greatest actors of the twentieth century, developed an approach to acting and

18 Sharon M. Carnicke, *Stanislavsky in Focus* (London and New York, Routledge, 1998), p. 139.

performing that affords the actor access to resources *within* himself or
herself that are based not merely in personal experience, but in the bridge
(the complete harmonization) between the body and psychology—the
psycho-physical connection. In his classic work *To the Actor*, Chekhov
describes the requirements for tapping into this connection:

> First and foremost is extreme *sensitivity of the body to the psychological*
> *creative impulses*...This brings us to the delineation of the second
> requirement, which is the *richness of the psychology itself*...The third
> requirement is *complete obedience of both body and psychology to*
> *the actor.* The actor who would become master of himself and his craft
> will banish the element of "accident" from his profession and create a
> firm ground for his talent. Only an indisputable command of his body
> and psychology will give him the necessary self-confidence, freedom
> and harmony for his creative activity. (pp. 1–5)
>
> —Michael Chekhov
in To the Actor

The tie that binds in this connection between the psychological and the
physical, as well as the spiritual—the connective tissue, the conduit, the
vehicle for transport—is BREATH.

> Artaud [1896–1948, the French playwright, poet, actor, director,
> and theorist] accepts that representation is inevitable in theatre, but
> intends to go beyond its chain of significations. Performativity, for
> him, is a temporal element of physical movement that reinforces the
> theatrical performance by the dynamics of breath...Only in the case of
> Artaud can we see the rejection of representation and the rediscovery
> of the "magic of breathing" in terms of an *active poetics* of theatre.
> When most of the thinkers of Artaud's time introduce movement in

philosophy and poetics as *repetition,* Artaud did separate repetition
from re-presentation by conceiving a different notion of performativity,
which is physical and non-conceptual. Inspired by a brief encounter
with Balinese rituals and performance traditions, myths and beliefs,
Artaud formulates a new means by which an actor can experience
higher levels of consciousness. This new means, for Artaud, is breath.
(p. 42)

—Sreenath Nair
in *Restoration of Breath*

THE BREATH CONNECTION: NEW LANGUAGE FOR FUNCTION

Breath, in both its functional and poetic definitions, is life-creating,
life-informing and, ultimately, life-defining. As Nair suggests in the
quote that opens this chapter, "the flow of breath is the flow of *presence*
and *absence* and therefore, the flow of breath is the flow of meaning.
Breathing is a movement that connects physical and mental activities
together and therefore, it is a movement of action, meaning, and
experience."

There are two basic activities associated with breath: inhalation
and exhalation. The detailed responsibilities of these primary functions
are much better described by the scientific community. Those of us
who count ourselves among "the living" are, arguably, experts at the
activity. But what if we add to this biological process the opportunity
to purposefully participate in the inherent relationship breath has with
expression? Perhaps a simple re-languaging of these basic terms can
evoke a more meaningful, and therefore more artistic, association with
the corresponding primary functions.

INHALATION, INSPIRATION... EXHALATION, EXPRESSION

As Bella Merlin states in *The Complete Stanislavsky Toolkit*, "Breathing (or 'respiration') is the rhythm of life, the sustainer of the human body, a fundamental tool for Stanislavsky in terms of acting processes...breath + rhythm = emotion:[19]

> Till you realize that the whole basis of your life—respiration—is not only the basis of your physical existence, but that *respiration plus rhythm forms the foundations of all your creative work,* your work on rhythm and breathing will never be carried out in full consciousness; that is to say, as it should be carried out, in a state of such complete concentration as to turn your creative work into "inspiration." (p. 98)

> —Konstantin Stanislavsky
> in *On the Art of the Stage*

> How does the actor act?...How can the actor learn to inspire himself? What can he do to impel himself toward that necessary yet maddeningly elusive creative mood? These were the simple, awesome riddles Stanislavski dedicated his life to exploring. Where and how to "seek those roads into the secret sources of inspiration must serve as the fundamental life problem of every true actor."
>
> "If the ability to receive the creative mood in its full measure is given to the genius by nature," Stanislavski wondered, "then perhaps ordinary people may reach a like state after a great deal of hard work with themselves—not in its full measure, but at least in part." (p. 36)

> —Foster Hirsch
> in *A Method to Their Madness*

---

19 Bella Merlin, *The Complete Stanislavsky Toolkit* (Hollywood, Drama Publishers, 2007), p. 34.

INHALATION/INSPIRATION

Inhalation—the in-taking of oxygen from the external environment—opens and exhilarates the instrument. It is also the performer's first step in the process that Nair coins as "bio-theatricality."[20] It is the "journey inward,"[21]...the moment in time that has the opportunity to visit thought, idea, opinion (conscious or subconscious)...the moment that occasions all that follows (musically, textually, and dramatically)... the precedent to expression...the moment when we as performers are truly *required*. Cicely Berry, voice director of the Royal Shakespeare Company, challenges performers to "root the voice" at the act of inhalation:

> What you are doing is reaching down to your centre for the sound. The breath goes in, and the sound comes out—you are touching down to your centre, you are finding the "I" of your voice. When you find this it is as though you belong, you are present in what you are saying. (p. 22)
>
> —Cicely Berry
> in *Voice and the Actor*

Regardless of the desired or needed *quantity*, the *quality* of the inhalation must be deep and full. If it is not its very nature, then it is certainly its *opportunity* to open areas of understanding and visit depth of feeling.

For musicians, much (if not all) of our expression is clearly defined for us. In fact, a portion of our "worth" is measured in how accurately

---

20 Sreenath Nair, *Restoration of Breath, Consciousness and Performance* (Amsterdam and New York, Rodopi B.V., 2007), pp. 46–47.
21 James Jordan and Nova Thomas, *Toward Center: The Art of Being for Musicians, Actors, Dancers, and Teachers* (Chicago, GIA Publications, 2010), p. 37.

we re-produce/re-present the page before us. Melodies are spelled, rhythm is delineated, harmonic settings are defined, dynamic markings and other interpretive "requests" are spelled, text (in the case of vocal music) is set, and there are often other musicians and a conductor to whom we are responsible as well. One could argue that there is little "room" for performers...that we are *reiterators* rather than creators. At best, it seems that we are vehicles for the intended expression of someone else.

Recently, at the conclusion of a particularly demanding lesson, a student asked me just where *she* might venture an interpretive opinion in the singing of an aria by Puccini (Giacomo Puccini was especially thorough in spelling out exactly what he wanted for singers to accomplish; and I had been vigilant in requiring of her the demands of the page). Performers often feel this way: there is much that they are responsible to. So then where, indeed, is our *voice*? Individuality, and the uniqueness that comes with it, is a birthright for each and every artist—every human being. The instrument itself is unique and *personality* has an undeniable presence in the utterance; but there is, via breath, and specifically inhalation, a place and moment in time to be *creative* as well.

Inhalation exists and functions as the "beat-before," the upbeat, the physical preparation before phonation. Artaud offers that for every thought or feeling that a character has, there is a corresponding breath that relates to and *precedes* its expression. It is in this very moment of inhalation, at this exact pulse of time, that we have the opportunity to *author* (at least *co-author*) that which is to follow. We create the reason and occasion the need. We *inspire* the expression. In those moments when we feel that the word is there because we *need* to say it...that the music is there because the performer or character *needs* to express some heightened state...then the seeds for authenticity are ours.[22]

For performers, there are many things that happen (that must happen) in order for the complicated functions of phonation, "musicing" (Dr. Jordan's term), and expression to occur. Some require conscious efforts, while others (a thankful majority) are products of the subconscious, habit, and rigorous practice. Most musicians are trained to remember and call upon, in the moment, the technical needs of craft; they are, however, less trained in the calling upon of those thoughts, ideas, and feelings that are associated with the creation of story and character-life—those triggers that function as the impetus and reason for the text and/or music that the composer and author have given us. If we can wrap our head and heart around *those* thoughts, and summon them in the rhythm and tempo that the music gives us in the "beat before," then craft and re-presentation will become art and a first-person experience/expression.

An Exercise to Assist the "Process"

As an exercise, I encourage singers and other musicians to mark every breath or "lift" before a new phrase. Then at those "breaths" I ask them to articulate and note a *logical* subtext (thought, idea, reaction, etc). Often I will suspend the tempo of the piece and ask the artist to speak the subtext before the phrase and/or defined expression it precedes. The exercise initially seems clumsy and contrived, but very quickly they find

22 James Jordan and Nova Thomas, *Toward Center: The Art of Being for Musicians, Actors, Dancers, and Teachers* (Chicago, GIA Publications, Inc., 2010), p. 44.

both the logic and the rhythm of precedent. With repetition one gains efficiency: the thought should ultimately last exactly (and only) as long as the composer allows.

It is also important to note that the subtext can change (in fact, it *should* change) according to both the internal and external given circumstances of any performance. The value of the exercise is that it creates a habit and experience for thinking *at all*. In this rhythm of thought-expression, spontaneity is not only possible, it is inevitable. Inhalation has indeed become the inspiration, and the performer becomes an empowered co-creator and author of the moment that it precedes.

ANIMATION AND INHALATION

Since inspiration is the moment in time, and provides the opportunity, for *creation*, it seems logical that it would also be the moment for "animation." Before going further, and derailing our attempts at authenticity in performance practice, it is prudent to be reminded of the real meaning of this word. The definition of the verb to "animate" harkens to the word origin associated with spirit and soul. It means "to give spirit to…to give life to".[23] In Jungian psychology, it references the true inner self. For the purposes of this discussion, rest assured that it has nothing to do with cartoonish behavior or "overacting." Actors live in fear of the criticism of "indicating." There are many nuances of meaning for this description associated with "bad acting," but the simplest can be found in the behaviors of overtly pointing to the objects

---

23 *animate*, def. Retrieved September 1, 2010, from http://dictionary.reference.com/browse/animate.

one is speaking about, or "mugging" with facial contortions that grotesquely describe feeling. At best, these undesirable and redundant behaviors are comical.

The discussion on exhalation/expression later in this chapter will iterate the many elements in music that are already in place to serve description. I would argue that these are quite enough: Music, especially music *with* text and the human voice, is one of the most effective methods of description and expression we have. Is it not, then, the thought that precedes expression, the inspiration, that might more organically summon animation or enlivening? In this rhythm of thought-expression, the expression *is* the action, or rather *re-action,* to what was visited and/or felt at the precedent moment of inhalation. Perhaps in simpler terms, the advice is to **"animate" the inspiration, and leave the expression to its own indigenous devices.**

REGARDING QUANTITY AND QUALITY

The oft-asked question of the *quantity* of air is certainly a topic of discussion and the focus of concern for many singers. I know firsthand the fine balancing act that navigates the travails of "too little or too much." Singing (in fact, all performing) is an athletic event, a "super-natural" phenomenon. Behaviors and practices that adequately serve everyday life are not, in my experience, "enough" for the kind of bio-theatricality Artaud, Stanislavsky, and Chekhov (among others) apostle. Commonplace function, involvement, and commitment do not yield the resonance (emotionally or audibly) that the theatrical space summons and requires. With this understanding in place, we are perhaps well-advised to consider the relationship of *quantity* to *quality*, and in doing so, define *quality* as worthy of our deeper considerations.

Cicely Berry presents a compelling argument for qualitative considerations (rather than quantitative) regarding the amount of air one needs at the inspiration. While Berry's focus-audience is actors responsible only to spoken (rather than sung) text, her thoughts are well worth consideration:

> We have to see the breath not simply as the means by which we make good sound and communicate information; but rather we have to see it as the physical life of the thought, so that we conceive the breath and the thought as one. We need to be able to encompass one thought with one breath. In everyday life we do not run out of breath in the middle of an idea—or seldom—so, even though the lengths of thought in a text are infinitely variable, this is what we should aim for. Unless we recognize that the breath and the thought are one, no amount of breathing exercises will give purpose to the breath, will make it organic to what we are saying.
>
> The further we go in getting this integration of breath and thought—and by thought I mean the utterance of a character charged with whatever feelings he may have—we begin to experience how the thought itself is moving, and the quality of the thought becomes active. We also see that how we share the breath is how we share the thought. If we waste the breath, we disperse and generalize the thought; and, conversely, if we hold on to the breath in some way, we reduce the thought by holding it back and locking it into ourselves. But, more important than this, we perceive that how we breath is how we think; or rather, in acting terms, how the character breathes is how the character thinks. The breath must encompass the thought, no more or less is needed: that is the precise energy of the thought.

If we think of breath in this way, and providing our capacity is good, we will always have enough. This is, of course, a little simplistic, and we obviously have to work at it as any athlete has to work at his supply of breath. We have to get to the point where the thought will control the breath....

I do believe that when we find this integration of thought and breath, when they are rooted down one with the other, the voice takes on a quite different and surprising energy, and the speaking becomes effortless. For, and this is what is important, we have made the thought our own physically through the breath, and so we do not have to press out our emotional and intellectual intentions.... (p. 26)

—Cicely Berry
in *The Actor and the Text*

The wonderful soprano, Christine Brewer is quoted as saying:

I have learned to breathe for the phrase, let the texts inspire the breath, and release the breath right before the beginning of each phrase rather than holding it. I used to take a huge breath for every phrase whether I need it or not. I learned that I needed to trust that my breath was going to carry me through each phrase.

—Christine Brewer
in W. Stephen Smith,
The Naked Voice

EXHALATION/EXPRESSION: LOCK OR LEAP?

Exhalation—the release of air from the lungs during the act of respiration—is, in our method of marrying breath with meaning, the carrier and delivery vehicle for all that was visited at the inspiration. It *is* the EXPRESSION.

While many schools of thought address the *management* of exhalation once the process of release has begun, it is in my experience and observation the *onset* of exhalation that needs the most attention. The moment when inhalation has completed its functional responsibilities— when inspiration has visited a thought, idea, or feeling that *needs* to be expressed—the instrument (and by "instrument" I mean mind, body, and spirit) typically, albeit usually momentarily, *locks*…at the very instant we would desire it to *leap*. Fears, judgments, and hesitations come in to "edit" and, in doing so, rob the spark of creativity. Even Artaud, a great advocate for the role of breath in expression, describes this very moment I reference as the "*frightful* transfer of forces from body to body."[24] Performers are most vulnerable here, but they are also at the threshold for authenticity. The great operatic tenor, Luciano Pavarotti, has been quoted as saying that singers are best served by thinking of sound as actually beginning at the end of inspiration, thus avoiding the awful moment of stiffening and constriction. Breath should be cyclic. The circle, to borrow from that great old hymn, should "be unbroken." The unedited onset of expression perhaps requires a courageous act of will; the alternative, a *withholding*, hijacks one's primary responsibility to share, to communicate.

It seems impossible for breath to escape the body without opinion. The respiratory system is the first system (or at least one of the first systems) that responds/reacts to an emotional impetus. Our own language is peppered with linguistic truths that reference the function as a describer of emotional states: it took my breath away, save your

---

24 Sreenath Nair, *Restoration of Breath, Consciousness and Performance* (Amsterdam and New York, Rodopi B.V., 2007), pp. 39–40.

breath, out of breath, hold your breath, in the same breath, under one's breath, with ragged breath, a breath of fresh air, don't breathe a word, to catch one's breath, to be left breathless, to get a second wind… and the list goes on and on. Nair referred to breath as "the invisible *Other* that reinforces meaning into performativity."[25] Once that "other" has begun its release, it seems impossible—for better or worse, but always "for real"—to edit its honest nature. It is indeed the moment of, and for, release that deserves commitment. But once release has begun, then what?

THE "S-WORD"

As a singer, addressing an audience that will certainly include other singers (and in spite of my commitment to *not* discuss the *technical* mechanics of function), I would be remiss not to mention what is perhaps the most misunderstood term in vocal terminology: *support*. It has been referred to as the "s-word."[26] Reid chronicles the fallacies of the idea and discusses the term as an invalid principle of function…a "suspect" pedagogic practice. The respected pedagogue, Richard Miller, in discussing *breath control* references many approaches as a calling upon of "disjunct anatomical information".[27] Nevertheless, every student, teacher, theorist, and practitioner spends a good bit of time dealing with it.

The best descriptions for consideration seem to re-language the practice—to reference it and understand it in terms of a *dynamic*

25 Sreenath Nair, *Restoration of Breath, Consciousness and Performance* (Amsterdam and New York, Rodopi B.V., 2007), pp. 39–40.
26 W. Stephen Smith, *The Naked Voice* (Oxford University Press, 2007), p. 39.
27 Richard Miller, *The Structure of Singing* (Schirmer, 1996), p. 278.

rather than a stiff upholding, or (least desirable) withholding, concept. Richard Miller discusses the desired *"dynamic muscular balance"* as follows:

> There is a historical pedagogical approach that drills the coordination needed for the demands of artistic vocalism. It goes by the name of *appoggio*, an international technique of breath management that, despite its Italianate name, crosses all national boundaries. This... approach is in contrast to either the "in-and-upper" or the "down-and-outer" schools of "breath support." *Appoggio*, as admirably described by Francesco Lamperti more than a century ago, had its origins in the pedagogical literature of the eighteenth- and nineteenth-century Italian School: the muscles of inspiration must not surrender too early to the muscles of expiration.... (p .77)

> —Richard Miller
> in *On the Art of Singing*

In the spirit imbuing functional terms with meaning, I and my colleagues Keith Buhl and Christopher Arneson would offer yet another descriptor for this idea. We three were authors of a curriculum of voice and speech training for the Actors Studio Drama School when it was part of the New School University in New York City. In an endeavor to make singing concepts usable and meaningful for actors and spoken text, we were often challenged to think of well-worn methods and "singer-isms" in new ways—ways that were pertinent and applicable to the actor's process. These efforts quickly became less of an exercise in adaptation and more of an opportunity for renewed life and practice in our own artistic processes. "Support" was one such area for focus. In an agreed-upon pedagogical practice of *appoggio*, we chose to identify the process as "a refusal to collapse."[28] This phrase achieved our goal of marrying terminology with instruction rather than description, and it interfaced with the actor's process and obligation for "doings." Just as a good actor would never relinquish the all-motivating character's objective, neither would the actor in our process to partner the needs of resonance collapse the "readied" and aligned body, the positioned pharynx, or the breath needed to deliver sound and expression to a waiting audience.

Scott McCoy, a renowned pedagogue and deeply committed educator for the relationship of scientific truths to effective teaching methods, simply and succinctly defines the singer's goal:

> Regardless of the specific method used, the goal of breath support…is to provide a stable supply of air at the correct pressure for the desired pitch and loudness.
>
> —Scott McCoy
> in *Your Voice: An Inside View*

---

28   Keith Buhl, Christopher Arneson, and Nova Thomas, *Voice and Speech for the Stanislavsky Actor: A Curriculum Manual for Teachers.* (unpublished manuscript)

IN SUMMARY

Great performers and great performances offer their blessed witnesses moments of magic. These magical results often lead one to believe that the process might be mystical. And in many ways, I suppose it is. But it is the intention of this book, and this now teaching artist, to find ways to demystify a process, a method, for creating the results that occasion the very magic we all find on those all-too-rare (but ever looming) nights in the theater. Quantifying a process for the performer doesn't necessarily compromise the effort. In fact, it empowers. Breath is a tool, the connective tissue between truth and its re-presentation. The audience's act of recognition depends upon the performer's integrity in, and commitment to, the carriage of ideas and feelings. The carrier is breath—it is both the performer's transport vehicle for the journey inward and the delivery system for the outward expression. It is soul. It is source. It is essence. It is story.

The miracle of inspiration and expression is, always and only, one breath away. And in those moments when the results of our efforts are less than perfect, well, so is redemption.

BIBLIOGRAPHY

Berry, Cecily. *The Actor and the Text.* New York City: Applause, 1987.

Berry, Cecily. *Voice and the Actor.* New York: Macmillan, 1973.

Buhl, Keith, Christopher Arneson, and Nova Thomas. *Voice and Speech for the Stanislavsky Actor: A Curriculum Manual for Teachers.* (unpublished manuscript)

Carnicke Sharon M. *Stanislavsky in Focus.* London and New York: Routledge, 1998.

Chekhov, Michael. *To The Actor.* New York: Routledge, 1953.

Hirsch, Foster. *A Method to Their Madness: The History of the Actors Studio.* New York: Da Capo Press, 1984.

Jordan, James, and Nova Thomas. *Toward Center: The Art of Being for Musicians, Actors, Dancers, and Teachers.* Chicago: GIA Publications, Inc., 2010.

Merlin, Bella. *The Complete Stanislavsky Toolkit.* Hollywood: Drama Publishers, 2007.

Miller, Richard. *The Art of Singing.* New York: Oxford University Press, 1996.

Miller, Richard. *The Structure of Singing.* New York: Schirmer, 1996.

Nair, Sreenath. *Restoration of Breath, Consciousness and Performance.* Amsterdam and New York: Rodopi B.V., 2007.

Reid, Cornelius L. *A Dictionary of Vocal Terminology: An Analysis*. New York: Joseph Patelson Music House, 1983.

Reid, Cornelius L. *Voice: Psyche and Soma*. New York: Joseph Patelson Music House, 1975.

Smith, W. Stephen. *The Naked Voice*. New York: Oxford University Press, 2007.

Stanislavsky, Konstantin. Translated by David Magarshack. *On the Art of the Stage*. London: Farber and Farber, 1973.

CHAPTER 16

QIGONG PRACTICE:
BALANCING ENERGY AND
GAINING AWARENESS OF BREATH

The three intentful corrections [1. Align the body, 2. Engage the breath, 3. Focus the mind], also know as the three regulations, the three adjustments, or the three focal points, are the bedrock of every form of Qigong and Tai Chi. You will notice that to take a deep breath, you must adjust your posture. You will notice that to adjust your posture, it helps to take a deep breath. Once you adjust the posture and the breath, it becomes natural to relax and clear the mind/consciousness. (p. 32)

—Roger Jahnke
in *The Healing Promise of Qi*

This is the first, wildest, and wisest thing I know, that the soul exists, and that it is built entirely out of attentiveness. (p. 34)

—Mary Oliver
from "Low Tide" in
The Amicus Journal

There are many ancient practices that can sensitize you to breath and its powers. The ancient meditative practice of Qigong is a practice that, if performed with regularity, will not only empower one's breath but also serve to keep the balance of energies within the body. Body, breath, and energy are all intimately interrelated. When practiced regularly, Qigong balances body, mind, and breath into a naturally functioning, aware, and organic whole.

The ancient Chinese practice of Qigong (pronounced *chee-gong*) has many different branches. For purposes of this text, I will present one particular practice. However, all of the various practices are worth investigation by any musician who values breath and the awareness of breath. I have found that even after one session of this ancient meditative and energy practice, I feel energized and renewed. And this practice has much in common with my training as a conductor. In fact, the skill for acquiring "Qi" (or energy) through this practice has proved to be a valuable daily tool for me in my work and my teaching. Aside from the valuable energy aspects of the art, there are many additional health benefits.

A QIGONG PRIMER FOR MUSICIANS: CULTIVATING QI

There can be no doubt about the various meditative/physical studies and/or practices that allow body, mind, spirit, and breath to maintain contact with each other. Yoga practitioners sing the praises of its constant practice and integration into one's lifestyle. Tae Kwon Do practitioners tout its benefit to overall mental and spiritual health, and its abilities to center oneself and one's energies. The practice of Alexander Technique has gained many musician practitioners because of the body awareness it teaches. Many musicians stumble into the benefits of these practices after they encounter some type of "stress" and "tension" that, in turn, impacts their music making through their inability to breathe.

I would like to present here a relatively new viewpoint on the use of the ancient practice of the Chinese healing practice of Qigong as just such a vehicle for all musicians.[29] Qigong seems to be one practice that not only leads to a replenishment of musician "energy stores" but also stabilizes the access of breath through acquisition and balancing of the energy of Qi in conjunction with breath.[30]

What is Qigong?

In my opinion, this phenomenon (of Qigong) can be compared with the launching and receiving principle in radio, for it is a special "field" in objective reality. If only you know how to receive Qi with the corresponding specific means, you can receive Qi to obtain its curing effect. (p. 68)

—Ou Wen Wei
in *Pan Gu Mystical Qigong*

If there is one concept that comes up in all forms of Chinese medicine it is that of Qi, or vital energy. Qi is the very backbone of the Chinese healing arts. It refers to the energy of the universe that is channeled from nature and runs through all of us. To have Qi is to be alive, while to have none is to be dead.

---

29 I was first introduced to this practice in Sedona, Arizona, at the MiiAmo Spa. After one class, I immediately felt the results of this relatively simple and direct approach taught by Paulette, who is on staff at the spa. I was impressed because many of its central principles were not only easily acquired in one class, but were also directly in line with the principles I believe are centrally important to the art of conducting and breathing.

30 My first familiarity with the term of Qi (pronounced *chee*) was in my acquaintance with a school of conducting pedagogy in Japan where there are a minimum number of gestures taught. All gestures are taught as movement toward or away from the "Qi." This Qi point is what has been referred to in the Western world as the "ictus."

Qi Gong also relies on the manipulation of this vital energy. This is done through "meridians," channels that pass through all the vital organs of the body. There are twelve of these meridians, which correspond to twelve organs. These meridians are interconnected, so that one runs intro the other and passes through the body like an invisible river of energy. Anyone can learn simple exercises to manipulate his or her own Qi. This practice is known as internal Qi Gong. (p. xiii)

The root of the way of life, of birth and change, is Qi; the myriad things of heaven and earth all obey this law. Thus Qi in the periphery envelops heaven and earth. Qi in the interior activates them. The source wherefrom the sun, moon and stars derive their light, the thunder, rain, wind and cloud their being, the four seasons and the myriad things their birth, growth, gathering and storing; all this is brought about by Qi. Man's possession of life is completely dependent upon this Qi. (p. 284)

—Hong Liu
in *The Healing Art of Qi Gong*

At the risk of over-simplifying the concepts of this practice, I have attempted to summarize both the practice of Qigong and its benefits to musicians.[31] Basically stated, the mind/body exercises advocated by this specific practice of Qigong allow the body to function in parallel as a type of radio device. Through Qigong, one learns to use the body as a "receiver" of energy or Qi that is constantly around us. This energy is carried in atoms and particles energized by the sun and moon, which are available for "collection." The exercises are the collection devices that allow us as musicians to recharge and refocus that have direct benefits upon our physical, mental, and spiritual health. Acquisition of Qi may be felt as vitality. At times, one can feel a certain magnetic or energy

31 I would encourage readers who are interested in acquiring the skills for this practice to not only find a practitioner in Qigong (reference website www.Pangushengong.org) but to read and study the concise book by Ou Wen Wei, *Pan Gu Mystical Qigong* (Burbank, CA: Unique Publications, 2008).

force between one's hands. Acquiring Qi possesses both conscious action and super-conscious action.

Again at the risk of sounding very New Age, Qigong aims at achieving within ourselves a certain balance and harmony of the energy that is *around* us and *within* us. The energy within us can only be replenished from sources that are external to us. Qigong provides us with a way of harvesting the energy that is omnipresent in the environment around us. The key to acquisition is a mind that is calm and a spirit that is open and loving. Finally, Qigong teaches body positions that maximize this energy acquisition. When these "energy centers" become rebalanced, the breath becomes deeper and more meaningful. Moreover, as one performs the Qigong exercises, the primary awareness that is gained is an intimate awareness and connection to one's breath.

ENERGY FLOW AND BREATH IN QIGONG

One of the most valuable images necessary in the practice of Qigong is the concept of energy and its connection to breath. This image is valuable for not only conductors but also all musicians. When visualizing the flow of energy throughout the body, visualize that the energy (and breath) flows through your *entire* body like water. This flow is constant, and its speed is directly relational to the amount of external energy that can be brought into the body. Stated another way, you must be in a constant state of awareness of your entire body for energy to flow throughout all parts of your body in this way. Unawareness leads to severe blockages in energy, which in turn will manifest themselves in human interaction problems and musical issues.

Qigong is another vehicle by which we as musicians can maintain a state of constant physical awareness. Physical awareness is the catalyst for spiritual awareness (to be discussed in the next section). The goal, it seems to me, is for musicians to acquire the skills by which energy acquisition becomes habitual. That feeling of liquid energy flow within the body is both a constant and a norm for our daily existence.

THE PATTERN OF ENERGY FLOW IN QIGONG

I have found that one of the most difficult concepts to impart to both my choirs and to conductors is how energy flows through the body. Many believe that the body is a vibrating mass of protoplasm—that energy, somehow, reaches the ensemble by sheer power of perception. Such a perception will certainly lead to a minimal transference of energy to ensemble, instrument, or audience.

Many others believe that energy is generated from a furnace-like source in the body, which is, almost literally, "hurled" or thrown out at the ensemble. Such a bombardment usually has the opposite effect. It creates a driven, aggressive sound in an ensemble. Such energy dispersion is also the product of persons who are unable to "let go" and trust themselves or their ensemble. They are personas who believe music "is made" rather than it being a reaction as a result of correct energy transference to an ensemble. They are perceived as being "energetic," but their energy generally has a detrimental effect upon the musicians they come in contact with. I have often observed in this type of person that such energy flow, because of its inward and cumulative effect, often breeds frustration. Energy held within becomes so powerful that it turns the person on himself or herself, and the result is frustration and a type of "nervousness" and impatience because the energy is not being used.

An analogy might be helpful: One of the older homes I lived in came equipped with a coal insert for the fireplace. This insert had sliding iron shutters on the front door to allow for proper ventilation of the coal fire. One time when I added coal to the fire, I neglected to open those vents. I left the room and returned about twenty minutes later, and the entire insert glowed red-hot! Not until I opened the vents and allowed heat out into the room did the metal cool to its normal color and state.

Musicians who do not practice or conceptualize the correct flow of energy constantly "overheat." This "overheating" needs to be eliminated from the body through some type of "cool down." Unfortunately, for many of us, we get rid of this overheated and misdirected energy in many negative ways.[32]

TWO PARADIGMS FOR ENERGY SHARING OR DISPERSION FOR MUSICIANS

There are two very helpful paradigms I have found in the energy dispersion process. In Qigong, one of the paths of energy through the body is called the "fire path.[33] The path runs down the center of the body from the forehead toward the outside of the body cavity, down through the pelvis, upward along the spine, around the back of the

---

32 The concept of mimetics certainly is a synonym for what is being described here. Conscious thought is similar to the vent doors in the coal furnace. Conscious thought of love and care begins to channel life energies in a positive direction to other musicians or the ensemble.

33 Yang Jwing-Ming, *The Root of Chinese Qigong* (YMAA Publication Center, 1997), p. 85.

skull, and completes its cycle over the top of the skull. This energy flow, if allowed to occur, is constant. Energy is then shared in two ways with other musicians. First, the most powerful transference of energy occurs from the circulation of energy that travels along the external core of the body. If the arms are used correctly by the conductor, the center of the body is left "open" for that energy to be sent and to be perceived by the ensemble. That energy is sensed like a vertical pillar or rod from the pelvis upward to the top of the head.[34] This is a powerful energy core that must be kept open and free as much as possible.

Second, other energy or Qi is transferred through the arms and out to the ensemble through the *palms* of the hands. This is possible because the arms are connected to the body energy circulation via the sternoclavicular joint.[35]

The proper perception of both of these paths of energy circulation are essential for the maintenance of a healthy "energy" and sharing of that energy (Qi) in a healthy way with your ensemble. Examine the illustration below and note the direction of the arrows, which detail the overall pattern of the energy flow throughout the body.

34 Also remember that the eyes are immediately adjacent to this pillar of energy and play their own role in the sharing of vital energies.
35 It is essential that the entire arm and its structure be understood and mapped if one desires appropriate energy flow to be shared with the ensemble.

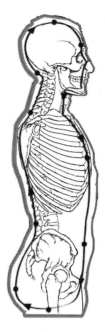

Pattern of Energy Circulation in the Body: Side View

THE BASIC QIGONG EXERCISE SEQUENCE:
THE TWENTY-SIX REPETITIONS

In this specific practice of Qigong, the following exercises are performed sequentially.[36] Slow and constant movement is the key to ample energy acquisition. Twenty-six repetitions are required for each movement. This number is based upon spiritual numerology. A verbal recitation at the beginning and end of the exercise sequence frames the entire repetition sequence.

---

36   For readers desiring additional detail, two sources should be consulted. The text *Pan Gu Mystical Qigong* by Wenwei Ou (Unique Publications, 2008) offers a detailed, step-by-step description of this approach to Qigong. This author also recommends visiting the website of the Pan Gu Shengong International Research Institute: www.pangushengong.org.

A prerequisite to all of these exercises is a sense of core body alignment. In my research and study, I have found that one can best find the core alignment of one's body through awarenesses gathered from sitting on an exercise ball.[37] Being organized like an apple around a core (the core being one's pelvis) is central to vital energy flow through the body. Without organizing your body around your core, it will be difficult, if not impossible, to experience the free flow of energy throughout your body. At all times during these exercises, you must maintain an awareness of your alignment and body core through constant body awareness. The following diagram is a necessary image for this to happen during the execution of the Qigong exercises.

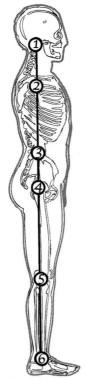

---

37   Reference *Learn Conducting Technique with the Swiss Exercise Ball (GIA, 2004)*.

BREATHING

You must also employ proper images for breathing at all times (as detailed in Chapter 6 of this book). Body Mapping, as demonstrated with the eight-handed breathing exercise, is central to this process. Throughout all of the exercises, it is important to remember that air comes into your body in a wave-like motion from top to bottom. Exhalation also occurs in a wavelike motion from top to bottom. This breathing technique attempts to wed breath with spirit. Obviously, such a technique would be beneficial to musicians.[38]

> Before we enter this practice, I must emphasize one more thing. That is the entire Embryonic Breathing practice occurs through self-inner-observation…That means "self-inner-feeling." This feeling is the way your mind communicates with your physical body, Qi and Shen. This feeling can be shallow or profound, depending on how much you are able to calm down your mind down and feel it. The level of feeling is unlimited, and normally follows the depth of your mind and awareness. Naturally, wrong feeling or mental perception can also lead you into fascination, illusion, and imagination. These false and unrealistic feelings can lead you to a state of emotional disturbance, and further away from the correct practice of Qi cultivation. (p. 323)
>
> —Yang Jwing-Ming
> in *Qigong Meditation*

---

38   For those interested in a deeper insight, reference Chapter 5, "The Practice of Embryonic Breathing," in *Qigong Meditation: Embryonic Breathing* (YMAA Publication Center, 2003) by Yang Jwing-Ming.

TEMPO OF THE EXERCISES

All exercises must be performed in a slow tempo, approximately between quarter = 42 and quarter = 60. The speed of the movement in the hands must be both constant and unvarying. It is the constant slow speed of the hand movements that allows you to feel and gather energy from the atmosphere surrounding your hands. Control and maintenance of a consistent speed is most important in the performance of the exercise sequence.

STARTING POSITION AND RECITATION

This position is most important. The palms up position of the hands allows for energy or Qi to enter your body and, in essence, recharge it. The belief is that energy enters the energy meridians of the body through the palms. Spend approximately two minutes in this position as you focus your thought on the breath, devoid of ego. To assist in getting ego out of the way, and beginning the proper flow of energy, many practitioners of Qigong encourage an out-loud recitation. This recitation, no matter its form, should include elements of giving, sharing, acquiring and love. For example:

Take kindness and benevolence as basis;
Take frankness and friendliness as bosom.
Speak with reason; Treat with courtesy;
Move with emotion; Act with result.[39]

---

39 Wenwei Ou from title page of *Pan Gu Mystical Qigong* (Unique Publications, 2008).

EXERCISE: LEFT SIDE MOTION

For this exercise, move to the position where the hands are parallel on the left side of the body. The hands should be no more than sixteen inches apart. Move the hands in a slow and circular clockwise motion, with the lower hand following the motion of the upper hand, but slightly behind the upper hand. Perform one complete rotation every two seconds. Twenty-six complete cycles should be performed.

Left Side Motion

Motion Transfer
from Left to Right

EXERCISE: MOTION TRANSFER FROM LEFT TO RIGHT

After the twenty-six rotations are completed, take both hands and move them to the center of the body, parallel with your navel. Transition the same position to the right side of the body. As you transition, the hand that was on the bottom is now on the top on the right side of the body.

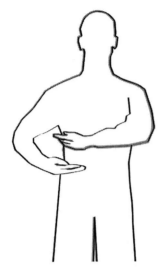

EXERCISE: RIGHT SIDE MOTION

Perform the same circular motion with the left hand on top, and right following it. Perform one complete rotation every two seconds. Twenty-six complete cycles should be performed.

Right Side Motion

EXERCISE: MIDDLE MOTION

After the motion has been completed on the right side of the body, turn your hands so they are parallel with the mid-line of your body, and rotate the hands, one following the other, for twenty-six forward rotations, with each rotation taking at least two seconds. The slower the rotations, the greater the benefit.

Middle Motion

EXERCISE: DRAWING OPEN MOTION

After you have completed the repetitions in middle motion, still your hands. Open your arms slowly while inhaling.

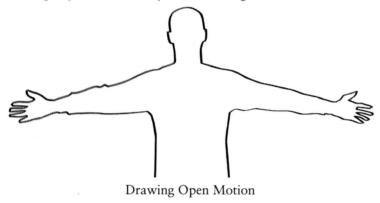

Drawing Open Motion

EXERCISE: DRAWING CLOSE MOTION

After exhaling and moving to the drawn open position, return to middle position while exhaling, arriving at a flower or "cupped" position of the hands.

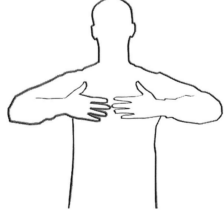

Drawing Close Motion

EXERCISE: FLOWER FOCUSING MOTION

After the drawing close motion, bring your hands into a cupped position, as if your hands are holding a flower. This hand position should mirror the position of your chin line and be approximately two to four inches below your chin. Stay in this position for approximately two minutes. If time permits, repeat the entire sequence again.

Flower Motion (Focusing Motion) and Recitation

CHAPTER 17

A FINAL ADMONITION:
BREATHE INTO THE IDEA

When your being is right, the doing will take care of itself.

> —Elaine Brown
> Alumni Lecture at
> Westminster Choir
> College, March 1989

For art to appear, we have to *disappear.* This may sound strange, but in fact it is a common experience. The elementary case, for most people, is when our eye or ear is "caught" by something: a tree, a rock, a cloud, a beautiful person, a baby's gurgling, spatters of sunlight reflected off some wet mud in the forest, the sound of a guitar wafting unexpectedly out of a window. Mind and sense are arrested for a moment, fully in the experience. Nothing else exists. When we "disappear" in this way, everything around us becomes a surprise, new and fresh. Self and environment unite. Attention and intention fuse. (p. 51)

> —Stephen Nachmanovitch
> in *Free Play*

This is an absolute truth I want you to embrace for the rest of your singing life. That's how confident I am about what I am telling you.

Hear it, breathe into THAT, and sing into THAT. Do not take a breath to sing; take a breath that is already the thought.

—Thomas Hampson
Westminster Choir
College master class
November 18, 2009

The thrill of a lifetime is to have a little child on your lap, they hold the Dr. Seuss book, or whatever book it is, and the pages open and you get very close to them at their ear and look over their shoulder and read what's there with warm breath and great meaning, and their little hands start rubbing the picture and it comes to life; that IS a glorious moment in time. You don't need music; that is the wonderment for that child.

But the audience, they are our children...and we have to reach them individually. And we have to mean it. They have to sense our integrity. And honesty...Artistic Truth.

—Paul Salamunovich
in *Chant and Beyond*

To trace the history of a river, or a raindrop, as John Muir would have done, is also to trace the history of the soul, the history of the mind descending and arising in the body. In both, we constantly seek and stumble on divinity, which, like the cornice feeding the lake and the spring becoming a waterfall, feeds, spills, falls, and feeds itself over and over again. (p. 72)

—Gretel Ehrlich
from "River History" in
Montana Spaces
in Yi-Fu Tuan, *Religion:*
From Place to
Placelessness

Beyond constant insecurities of busy-ness and emotion, in which we are worse off than any other animal, we have the gift of conscious penetration into the realms of our art, as the highest representative of our capacity to dream. (p. 6)

—Rudolf Laban
from "Education
through the Arts,"
April, 1957 in *Rudolf*
Laban Speaks about
Movement and Dance

Truly musical phrasing is musical *thought* in sound. Rationalized phrasing has the potential to reach far deeper into the psyche of the listener than performance based only on instinct, however good that instinct may be. (p. 1)

—David McGill
in *Sound in Motion*

Relationships—not facts and reason—are the key to reality. By
entering those relationships, knowledge of reality is unlocked.
(p. 119)

—Parker Palmer
as quoted by William
Sloane Coffin
in *Credo*

While this book addresses the intrinsic power of the breath for
all musicians, because I am a conductor, I come to this book wanting
to share a message that needs to be heeded, or at least entertained,
by those who conduct musicians who need to breathe to create their
art. For some reason, it seems conductors either do not breathe or, if
they do, their breath is not readable by others spiritually, physically, or
both. To say that not to empower breathing is a musical handicap is an
understatement.

UNDERSTANDING THE POWER OF THE BREATH

Our business in life is less making something of ourselves than finding
something worth doing and losing ourselves in it. (p. 126)

—William Sloane Coffin
in *Credo*

I have always found that if paradigms are clear in one's mind,
then one can operate almost at an instinctual level. For the breath to
function as I believe it can function, one must believe that it possesses
such power and then be submissive through one's profound belief that

the breath can do all that it can do. It is one's belief and the "allowing" that empowers each breath to carry human and musical content into the sounds that grow out of that breath. One must spend much time pondering the power of breath.

THE BREATH IS A SUBMISSIVE ACT

The great oboist Marcel Tabuteau, whose approach to shaping influenced an entire generation of musicians (and, to this day, his influence is felt at The Curtis Institute) Tabuteau believed that "I have always been in favor to play as I think. Of course, the ideal combination would be to play with *thinking* and *intelligent feeling*. If you think beautifully, you play beautiful [*sic*]. I believe to play as you think more than to play as you feel because how about the day you are not feeling well?"[40]
And how does one "think"? Through the breath!

Recent studies on Somatics (and one of its branches, Body Mapping), has provided us with powerful proof that other musicians will only perceive what *you* perceive. That is, if you do not perceive your breath, and do not infuse your breath with musical intention and idea, then others will never be able to "read" your ideas.

For singers, the idea will not be in the sound; for conductors, a serious breach in communication of musical idea and human connection will take place. For musicians, human connection is part human, part musical idea. For conductors, the strength of the communicative power of an ensemble is directly proportional to how the breath is empowered

---

40   David McGill, Sound in Motion (Indiana University Press, 2007), p. 17.

by the conductor. If you are not aware of your breath and its content, then a world of communication is lost to your ensemble.

Conductors who are unable to employ breath as one of their "tools" end up believing that conducting technique and efficient rehearsal technique can solve all musical issues. Conducting technique takes care of detail. Vocal technique and instrumental technique take care of detail. As a conductor you must take care of musical detail. However, you must also understand that technique cannot carry the idea. That idea must be spontaneously provided. Good technique and musical detail allow musical idea to live. But breath, and breathing into the idea, and then making the musical idea audible is the miracle of not only conducting, but all musical performance.

How this is accomplished in our humanness denies clear and perhaps objective explanation. It is not a simple matter to explain the particular miracle of breath. It is a miracle, to be accepted. The closest I can come to describing the experience is that at the moment of breath, one breathes into an idea and becomes totally submissive to the power that is in the breath—no questioning, no logic, no reasoning, no cognitive control, just total submission at that breathing moment to the totality of the breath and its powers.

The power of the breath has been acknowledged by major religions, philosophic thought, and various physical disciplines, including Yoga, Tai Chi, Qigong, etc. In Hebrew, *Ruach* has two meanings: spirit *and* breath. In Chinese, Chi means both energy *and* breath. In the Roman Catholic faith, at the Chrism Mass celebrated during Holy Week, the bishop mixes the sacred chrism into the olive oil and before saying the prayer of blessing breathes on the oil (harking back to Jesus breathing on the disciples and God breathing over the chaos). It is the *Ruach,* the Holy Sprit, that comes through the breath of the bishop and consecrates the sacred Chrism. The Chrism essence is also a mixture of fragrant oils, the sense of smell being intimately related to breathing. I suppose you could take this one step further by saying that you cannot possibly create without breath. It is breath and the spirit in that breath—*Ruach*— that creates.

THE "TRINITY" DILEMMA OF THE ARTIST

If you believe at any level in the miracle of the creative process, then an awareness of the role breath must have in that process must be part of that belief. It is part belief, part awareness in what the breath carries. This belief can be traced back as early as Aristotle. Aristotle went to great lengths to connect breath into fundamental life experiences. Aristotle believed that it was breath that was the link between mind and body.

> Considering the value of the argument that Aristotle establishes in terms of breath and its psycho-physical movements, it is obvious that each physical movement and each mental reflection must have a corresponding movement of breath in the body, linking physical activities and mental experiences together. For Aristotle, breath is the pure substance of the body that activates the process of respiration, and all the psycho-physical movements including emotions and physical animations are the results of the dynamics of breath in the body. (p. 57)
>
> —Sreenath Nair
> in *Restoration of Breath*

At the beginning of the twentieth century, Dorothy Sayers, an Anglican theologian, had not only deeply unique insights into the artist's dilemma, but also an explanation for the "letting go" process that must happen within the miracle of the breath for artists:

> For every work (or act) of creation is threefold, an earthly trinity to match the heavenly.
>
> First (not in time, but merely in order of enumeration) there is the Creative Idea, passionless, timeless, beholding the whole work complete at once, the end in the beginning: and this is the image of the Father.
>
> Second, there is the Creative Energy (or Activity) begotten of that idea, working in time from the beginning to the end, with sweat and passion, being incarnate in the bonds of matter: and this is the image of the Word.
>
> Third, there is the Creative Power, the meaning of the work and its response in the lively soul: and this is the image of the indwelling Spirit.
>
> And these three are one, each equally in itself the whole work, whereof none can exist without other: and this is the image of the Trinity.
> (p. 28)

—Dorothy L. Sayers
from her play, "The Zeal of Thy House"
in *Mind of the Maker*

The creative life of the artist can be viewed as functioning on three interactive levels—a Trinity of Creation, of sorts. One part of the artist studies scores for the composer's muse and message; the other part of the artist develops the details of his/her technique. But it is the third part of this Trinity that is the "allowing" part of the creative act. It is the "that" which we entrust to our breath, and trust that our work on

Chapter 17   A FINAL ADMONITION

the other parts of our creative Trinity will come into some type of union within our breath.

The creative idea is the most elusive and the most powerful. This creative idea defies cognitive control but works best when it is "allowed" to happen in the breath (a giving into the breath in the most totally uncontrolled submission to that breath that is humanly possible). Just as we learn to trust higher powers, we must learn as artists to trust in the breath. Trusting this mystery—that within our breath we can transport the "that" which is our idea and our spirit into every sound that follows—must be the life of every creative artist and teacher.

Antonin Artaud, the great liberator of the modern theater and actor, called the breath and all things connected to breath as a "magical act";[41] that breath does not freeze artistic expression "in the moment" but rather *transforms* the present into another real present that is not the future. That is surely heady stuff for consideration, but it highlights the fact that breath keeps artistic expression and artistic ideas honest and connected to those who are listening.

The breath and breathing with intention followed by submission into a force larger than ourselves will give rise to an honest and authentic musical voice. That voice, birthed in meaningful breath, will compel, move, and carry the composer's message in a way that will enrich all our lives. Perhaps the passage from Ecclesiasticus best summarizes our hopes for breath:

---

41 Sreenath Nair in *Restoration of Breath*, p. 173.

The wisdom of a learned man cometh by opportunity of leisure and he that hath little business shall become wise.

How can he get wisdom that holdeth the plough, and that glorieth in the goad, that driveth oxen, and is occupied in their labours, and whose talk is of bullocks?

He giveth his mind to make furrows; and is diligent to give the kine fodder.

So every carpenter and workmaster, that laboureth night and day; and they that cut and grave seals, and are diligent to make great variety, and give themselves to counterfeit imagery, and watch to finish a work:

The smith also sitting by the anvil, and considering the iron work, the vapour of the fire wasteth his flesh, and he fighteth with the heat of the furnace: the noise of the hammer and the anvil is ever in his ears, and his eyes look still upon the pattern of the thing that he maketh; he setteth his mind to finish his work, and watcheth to polish it perfectly:

So doth the potter sitting at his work, and turning the wheel about with his feet, who is always carefully set at his work, and maketh all his work by number;

He fashioneth the clay with his arm and boweth down its strength before his feet, ; he applieth himself to lead it over; and he is diligent to make clean the furnace:

192

All these trust to their hands: and every one is wise in his work. Without these cannot a city be inhabited: and they shall not dwell where they will, nor go up and down:

They shall not be sought for in public counsel, nor sit high in the congregation: they shall not sit on the judges' seat, nor understand the sentence of judgment; they cannot declare justice and judgment; and they shall not be found where parables are spoken.

But they will maintain the state of the world, and all their desire is the work of their craft.

—Ecclesiasticus xxxviii:24–34

About the Authors

JAMES JORDAN

James Jordan is considered to be one of the most influential choral conductors and educators in America. His over thirty publications, including books covering rehearsal and teaching pedagogy, conducting technique, and the spirituality of musicing, as well as numerous DVDs and recordings, have brought about far-reaching pedagogical and philosophical changes not only in choral music but also in the worlds of orchestral conducting, wind conducting, piano, and music education. *The Choral Journal* has described his writings as "visionary." Renowned American composer Morten Lauridsen dedicated the third movement of his *Midwinter Songs* to him.

One of the country's leading choral artists, Dr. Jordan is Senior Conductor at Westminster Choir College of Rider University, where he conducts the Westminster Williamson Voices and the Westminster Schola Cantorum, and teaches undergraduate and graduate choral conducting. Over thirty works have been premiered by the Westminster Williamson Voices, including the works of Mantyjaarvi, Custer, Ames, Hill, Whitbourn, Henson, and Wilberg. Dr. Jordan also conducts Anam Cara (www.anamcarachoir.com), a professional choral ensemble based in Philadelphia that has received critical acclaim for its recordings.

The *American Record Review* wrote that Anam Cara "is a choir to please the fussiest choral connoisseur" and called their inaugural recording, *Innisfree,* "skillful and shining," "glowing," "supremely accomplished" with a "tone that produces a wide range of effects from vocal transparency to rich, full-throated glory."

Dr. Jordan is one of the country's most prolific writers on the subjects of the philosophy of music making and choral teaching. His trilogy of books on the philosophy and spirituality of musicing—*The Musician's Soul, The Musician's Spirit,* and *The Musician's Walk*—have made a deep and profound impact upon musicians and teachers around the world. Dr. Jordan is also Executive Editor of the *Evoking Sound Choral Series* (GIA), which now includes over one hundred published works. In addition, he delivers over thirty workshops and keynote addresses each year in addition to an extensive conducting schedule.

Dr. Jordan has had the unique privilege of studying with several of the landmark teachers of the twentieth century. He was a student of Elaine Brown, Wilhelm Ehmann, and Frauke Haasemann. He completed his Ph.D. in Psychology of Music under Edwin Gordon. He has been the recipient of many awards for his contributions to the profession. He was named Distinguished Choral Scholar at The University of Alberta. He was made an honorary member of Phi Mu Alpha Sinfonia in 2002 at Florida State University.

Dr. Jordan's lecture/teaching schedule and writings are detailed on his Web site (www.evokingsound.com) and his publisher's Web site (www.giamusic.com/jordan).

MARK MOLITERNO, MM, RYT

Mark Moliterno holds BM and MM degrees in Voice and Opera from the Oberlin Conservatory of Music, where his mentor was the famous vocal pedagogue, Richard Miller. He subsequently continued his formal music studies at Rutgers University, University of North Carolina at Greensboro, the Britten-Pears School for Advanced Musical Study in Aldeburgh, England, and the Hochschüle für Musik, Mozarteum in Salzburg, Austria. He has enjoyed, and continues to maintain, an extensive performing career in opera, concert, and solo recital while being committed to his true passion and life's work as an educator.

Mr. Moliterno was first introduced to Hatha yoga in 1985 and has studied both viniyoga and classical hatha yoga. He is a certified yoga instructor through the YogaLife Institute of Pennsylvania. His yoga mentor is Robert Butera, PhD.

As an Adjunct Associate Professor of Voice at Westminster Choir College of Rider University, Mr. Moliterno teaches private voice and yoga for a wide range of students and educational programs. During the summers, he is a faculty member of the CoOPERAtive program and the High School Vocal Institute. He is also a member of the teaching staff at the YogaLife Institute in Devon, PA. As a natural outgrowth of his background, interests, and expertise, he has developed YogaVoice™, the application of classical yoga principles and practices for the lives and work of performing artists. YogaVoice™ seminars and training sessions are conducted in day-long, weekend, and week-long intensives around the country.

To contact Mr. Moliterno or for more information about his work and lecture/teaching schedule, e-mail yogavoice@gimail.com.

NOVA THOMAS

Nova Thomas is Assistant Professor of Voice at Westminster Choir College of Rider University and Professor of Professional Practice (Departmental Chair) at the New School for Drama, New School University (formerly the renowned Actors Studio Drama School) in New York City. Her many and varied teaching responsibilities include private vocal instruction, dramatic coaching, four progressive semesters of classes for the singing-actor, role preparation, a graduate course in Bel Canto literature, and advanced classes in voice and speech training. She is a recipient of the New School University's most prestigious award for "Excellence in Teaching" and is a highly sought-after master class teacher and speaker. Recent venues have included the Midwest Clinic (an international conference), National NATS and National Opera Association Winter Conference, an OPERA America-sponsored event on the training of big voices, and several university master classes. Additionally, she is a teaching artist and dramatic coach for Westminster Choir College's CoOPERAtive Program, a teaching artist for the University of Houston's and Texas Music Festival's *Le Chiavi di Bel Canto,* and a co-teacher with renowned actor and Tony Award winner Denis O'Hare in a series of master classes focused on the synthesis of vocal, musical, and dramatic techniques.

As a performer, Ms. Thomas is an internationally acclaimed soprano whose work has been consistently characterized as "ravishing in sound and magical in stage presence" (OPERA/London). International appearances have taken her to the opera houses of Cologne, Hamburg, Stuttgart, Paris, London, Dublin, Belfast, Mexico City, and Hong Kong. In the United States she has performed with the opera companies of New York City, Philadelphia, Santa Fe, Seattle, Baltimore, Detroit, San Diego, Indianapolis, St. Louis, Louisville, Knoxville, Houston, Memphis, Grand Rapids, Nashville, Costa Mesa, New Jersey, El Paso, Syracuse, and Anchorage (among others). Concert engagements have included performances with the Chicago Symphony, Cincinnati Symphony, and Indianapolis Symphony. Her repertoire features the heroines of *La Traviata, Il Trovatore, Norma, Otello, Aida, Un Ballo in Maschera, Tosca, Madama Butterfly, Il Trittico, Macbeth, La Boheme, Faust, Cosi fan Tutte, Le Nozze di Figaro, Anna Bolena, Don Giovanni, Turandot, Dialoques des Carmelites,* and *Les Contes d'Hoffman.* She has enjoyed a close collaboration with Dame Joan Sutherland and Maestro Richard Bonynge—the latter with whom she recorded the title role in *the Bohemian Girl* for Decca Records.

Her contribution to *The Musician's Breath* marks Ms. Thomas' second collaboration with James Jordan and GIA Publications. Their book, *Toward Center: The Art of Being for Musicians, Actors, Dancers, and Teachers*, with a foreword by James Conlon, was published in 2009.

Ms. Thomas is originally from North Carolina, where she received her home state's Lifetime Achievement Award for her contributions to the arts. She serves with General Henry Hugh Shelton, the former Chair of the Joint Chiefs of Staff, as a member of his board of directors for a national leadership initiative.

Bibliography

Adams, John. *Hallelujah Junction: Composing an American Life*. New York: Picador, 2008.

Aristotle. *On the Soul, Parva Naturalia, On Breath*. Translated by W. S. Hett. Cambridge, MA: Harvard University Press, Reprinted, 1957.

Bernstein, Leonard. *The Joy of Music*. Milwaukee, WI: Hal Leonard, 2004.

Berry, Cecily. *The Actor and the Text*. New York City: Applause, 1987.

————. *Voice and the Actor*. New York: Macmillan, 1973.

Blocker, Robert. *The Robert Shaw Reader*. New Haven, CT: Yale University Press, 2004.

Blum, David. *Casals and the Art of Interpretation*. Berkeley: The University of California Press, 1977.

Buhl, Keith, Christopher Arneson, and Nova Thomas. *Voice and Speech for the Stanislavsky Actor: A Curriculum Manual for Teachers*.

Bunch, Meribeth. *Dynamics of the Singing Voice*. Springer-Verlag: New York, 1982.

Camera, Gary Bede. *The Tao of Musicianship: 24 Meditations for the Musician Within Us*: Based Upon the "Tao Te Ching." Manchester, NH: Saint Anselm Abbey, 2001.

Cameron, Julia. *The Sound of Paper: Starting from Scratch*. New York: Penguin, 2004.

Campbell, Don G. *Master Teacher: Nadia Boulanger*. Washington, DC: The Pastoral Press, 1984.

Campbell, Joseph. *The Power of Myth*. New York: Doubleday, 1988.

Carnicke Sharon M. *Stanislavsky in Focus*. London and New York: Routledge, 1998.

Chekhov, Michael. *To The Actor*. New York: Routledge, 1953.

Coffin, William Sloan. *Credo*. Louisville, KY: Westminster John Knox Press, 2004.

Colgrass, Michael. *My Lessons with Kumi: How I Learned to Perform with Confidence in Life and Work*. Moab, UT: Real People Press, 2000.

Conable, Barbara. *How to Learn the Alexander Technique*. Columbus, OH: Andover Press, 1992.

———. *The Structures and Movement of Breathing*. Chicago: GIA Publications, 2000.

Copland, Aaron. *Music and Imagination*. Boston, MA: Harvard University Press, 1952.

———. *What to Listen for in Music*. New York: New American Library, 1985.

Crowe, Barbara. *Music and Soul Making: Toward a New Theory of Music Therapy*. Toronto: The Scarecrow Press, 2004.

De Waal, Ester. *The Way of Simplicity: The Cistercian Tradition*. Maryknoll, NY: Orbis Books, 1998.

Ehmann, Wilhelm. *Choral Directing*. Minneapolis, MN: Augsburg, 1968.

Eustis, Lynn. *The Singer's Ego*. Chicago: GIA Publications, 2005.

Farhi, Donna. *The Breathing Book*. New York: Henry Holt and Company, 1996.

Gallway, W. Timothy. *The Inner Game of Tennis*. New York: Random House, 1977.

Gordon, Edwin E. *Learning Sequences in Music*. Chicago: GIA Publications, 2007.

———. *Preparatory Audiation, Audiation, and Music Learning Theory*. Chicago: GIA, 2001.

Griliches, Diane Asseo. *Teaching Musicians: A Photographer's View*. New Hampshire: Bunker Hill Publishing, 2008.

Hendricks, Gay. Conscious Breathing. New York: Bantam Books, 1995.

Herbert, Rembert. *Entrances: Gregorian Chant in Daily Life*. New York: Church Publishing Incorporated, 1999.

Hirsch, Foster. A Method to Their Madness: The History of the Actors Studio. New York: Da Capo Press, 1984.

Hodgson, John, and Valerie Preston-Dunlop. *Rudolf Laban: An Introduction to His Work and Influence*. Plymouth, Great Britain: Northcote House: 1990.

Houston, Lisa. "An Interview with Thomas Hampson: Playing Your Game." *San Fransisco Classical Voice*, September 29, 2009.

Huther, Gerald. *The Compassionate Brain*. Boston, MA: Trumpeter, 2004.

Jordan, James, and Nova Thomas. *Toward Center: The Art of Being for Musicians, Actors, Dancers, and Teachers*. Chicago: GIA Publications, 2010.

Koch, Christoph. *The Quest for Consciousness: A Neurobiological Approach*. Englewood, CO: Roberts and Company Publishers, 2004.

McGill, David. *Sound in Motion*. Bloomington, IN: Indiana University Press, 2007.

Merlin, Bella. *The Complete Stanislavsky Toolkit*. Hollywood, CA: Drama Publishers, 2007.

Miller, Richard. *The Art of Singing*. New York: Oxford University Press, 1996.

———. *The Structure of Singing*. New York: Schirmer, 1996.

Moore, Thomas. *Care of the Soul*. New York: HarperPerrenial, 1994.

Nachmanovitch, Stephen. *Freeplay: Improvisation in Life and Art.* New York: Penguin Putnam, Inc., 1990.

O'Shaughnessy, Ann, and Roderick MacIver. *Art as a Way of Life.* North Ferrisburg, VT: Herron Dance Press, 2006

Palmer, Parker J. *The Active Life.* San Francisco, CA: Jossey-Bass, 1990.

Parker, Alice. *The Anatomy of Melody.* Chicago: GIA Publications, 2006.

Rama, Swami, Rudolph Ballentine, MD, and Alan Hymes, MD. *Science of Breath: Practical Guide.* Honesdale, PA: Himalayan Institute Press, 1998.

Reid, Cornelius L. *A Dictionary of Vocal Terminology: An Analysis.* New York: Joseph Patelson Music House, 1983.

———. *Voice: Psyche and Soma.* New York: Joseph Patelson Music House, 1975.

Rinpoche, Yongey Mingyur. *The Joy of Living.* New York: Harmony Books, 2007.

Rosenberg, Larry. *Breath by Breath: The Liberating Practice of Insight Meditation.* Boston, MA: Shambhala, 1998.

Saint Isaac the Syrian. *The Ascetical Homilies of Saint Isaac the Syrian.* Boston, MA: Holy Transfiguration Monastery, 1984.

Salamunovich, Paul. *Chant and Beyond.* Houston, TX: Quaid Schott Media Productions.

Sayers, Dorothy L. *Mind of the Maker*. New York: Mowbray, 1941.

Sommerfeldt, John R. *The Spiritual Teachings of Bernard of Clairvaux*. Kalamazoo, MI: Cistercian Publications, 1991.

Stanislavsky, Konstantin. *On the Art of the Stage*. Translated by David Magarshack. London: Farber and Farber, 1973.

Smith, W. Stephen, *The Naked Voice*. New York: Oxford University Press, 2007.

Thoreau, Henry David. *Where I Lived and What I Lived For*. New York: The Penguin Group, 2006.

Todd, Mabel E. *The Thinking Body*. Hightstown, NJ: Princeton Book Company, 1937.

Todd, Richard. *The Thing Itself: On the Search for Authenticity*. New York: Riverhead Books, 2008.

Tuan, Yi-Fu. *Religion: From Place to Placelessness*. Chicago: The Center for American Places, 2009.

Ullman, Lisa. *Rudolf Laban Speaks about Movement and Dance*. Woburn Hill, Addelstone, Surrey: Laban Art of Movement Centre, 1971.

Wakin, Daniel J. "A Conductor Whose Worship Stands Apart." *The New York Times*, February 21, 2010, p. 29.

Yogi Ramacharaka. *Science of Breath*. Chicago: Yogi Publication Society, 1905.

Symbols

Japanese reiki, symbol for breath

alchemy, symbol for spiritus

closed eye, symbol for ignorance

Ypsilon Cross, symbol for life choices

fish hook, Polynesian symbol for intention

bird, representing the soul

symbol for breath spiraling in and out of the body

symbol for breath defining an interior

the fountain, or butterfly, symbol for creativity, which cannot be contained

symbol for audiation

symbol for wave-like breath

symbol for living in the moment

symbol for a pause or silence in the musical soul

symbol for connection

symbol for OM

symbol for the flow of breath

symbol for balance, yin and yang

symbol for seed of life, representing creativity